# DIGNITY & INCLUSION

## Making it work for children with behaviour that challenges

Edited by Amanda Allard, Jan Delamore and Jeanne Carlin.
With Viv Cooper, Gemma Honeyman, Joy Beaney, Kay Al-Ghani,
Ian Townsend and Wendy Lee

**Our vision**

CDC's vision is a society in which disabled children's life chances are assured, their needs met, their aspirations supported and their rights respected.

**Our values**

We believe that:

- disabled children and young people should enjoy the same rights and opportunities as other children

- all disabled children and young people communicate and have a right to have their views heard

- the views of disabled children, young people and their families are vital to the development of an inclusive society

- all disabled children and young people should be fully included in every aspect of society.

Published by the National Children's Bureau

National Children's Bureau, 8 Wakley Street, London EC1V 7QE
Tel: 0207 843 6000
Website: www.ncb.org.uk
Registered charity number: 258825

NCB works in partnership with Children in Scotland (www.childreninscotland.org.uk) and Children in Wales (www.childreninwales.org.uk).

© National Children's Bureau 2014

ISBN: 978 1 907969 54 6

British Library Cataloguing in Publication Data
A catalogue record for this book is available from the British Library

The views expressed in this book are those of the authors and not necessarily those of the National Children's Bureau.

Typeset and printed by Fertile Creative, UK

# Contents

Foreword     i

**1. Introduction**     **1**
Define the children     1
Prevalence     3
How autism might affect learning and behaviour     4
Partnership with parent and children     5
Checklist for inclusion     6

**2. Balancing right, benefits and risks – policy and legislation**     **9**
Introduction     9
Effective risk management     9
Risk     10
Health and safety responsibilities     10
Rights of Access     12
Legislation and judgement     12
Entitlement to services     15
Inspection and registration     19

**3. Current practice**     **21**
Overcoming the barriers     21
Guidance     21
The place of disabled children in society     20
Process and practical issues     23
Conclusion     31
Book references     33
Second volume     34

**4. Partnership arrangements, joint policies and protocols**     **41**
Why is a partnership arrangement at an area level needed?     41
Who should be involved?     42
Monitoring and updating the policies and procedures     42
Using Continuing Healthcare funding     44
Adopting individual policy and procedures     44
What should the policy contain?     45
Supporting children who have behaviour that challenges
and safeguarding     46

**5. Working in partnership with parents and carers**     **57**
    Introduction and general principles     57
    Diversity     58
    Working together     58
    Developing a good relationship and partnership working     59
    Sharing information     59
    Regular communication with parent/carer     61
    Consent to behaviour plans     61
    Other forms of consent     62
    Maintaining the partnership     63
    Conclusion     63

**6. Promoting a partnership with the child**     **65**
    Consultation     65
    Process of decision making     67
    Children and young people giving consent     69
    Consent - information sharing     72

**7. Plans**     **75**
    Written records     76
    Written information     77
    Review     79

**8. Positive behaviour support plans**     **83**
    Positive behaviour support     85
    Developing a positive behaviour support plan     85
    Input from those who support the child     86
    Functional assessment of the behaviour(s)     87
    A proactive plan     88
    A reactive plan     90
    A review process     91
    Checklist for developing and implementing a positive behaviour
    support plan     91
    Organisational approach to positive behaviour support     92
    Risk assessment to support inclusion     106
    The elements in risk management     106
    Addressing fears about managing risk     107
    'Think safety'     107
    Use of equipment     108
    The general and the specific     108
    Specific policies     112

**9. Communication**     **115**
    Why communication?     115
    What do we mean by communication?     115
    The adult's role     116
    Communication needs     116

Difficulties with social interaction 120

General good practice 120

General strategies 122

Communication is a skill 122

Interventions 123

Practical ways of working with alternative communication methods 123

Examples of alternative and augmentative communication 123

Training/workforce development 124

**10. Training** **141**

Working with parents 141

Basic awareness training 144

Advanced training including restrictive physical interventions 145

Training in communication 146

Training in moving and handling 146

Safeguarding 147

**11. Written information** **151**

**12. Written records** **155**

**13. Conclusion and checklist** **157**

Checklist for inclusion 157

**Acknowledgements** **164**

# Foreword

The special educational needs and disability (SEND) reform programme signalled by the 'Support and Aspiration' Green Paper and mapped out in the Children and Families Act 2014 underlines the government's commitment to ensuring that every child achieves the best possible educational and life outcomes and is included in effective preparation for their adult life.

Whilst there are excellent examples of good practice as evidenced in this book we know that this group of children is one which services often struggle to meet the needs of successfully. Disabled children and their families have to be confident that services can meet their needs, with staff also feeling that they have the skills and resources to meet those needs.

This practical guidance for children with challenging behaviour is published alongside the SEND reforms. It will help services and settings to plan for and meet the needs and aspirations of these children more effectively and thereby, enable a far greater proportion to live within their own communities.

It is full of practical suggestions and solutions for positively engaging and including children who have challenging behaviour as a result of learning disability and or autism. There is also a wealth of resources such as risk assessments, behaviour management plans and communication passports.

It is vital that services and settings have a greater understanding about the needs of this particular group of children and how best to meet them, in particular that they understand behaviour as a form of communication. This volume will prove a useful tool in promoting such understanding and enabling both staff and service providers to develop activities and services which all children are able to benefit from.

**Edward Timpson, MP**

Parliamentary Under Secretary of State for Children & Families

# 1. Introduction

This publication will help all service providers to ensure that disabled children and young people can access services and lead a life as part of their local community. The information draws on examples of good practice from across the country. These examples illustrate the ways in which all agencies can work together to develop local policies and procedures to ensure that the needs of disabled children are met in a coordinated and child-centred way.

This is one of two companion publications that detail good practice in both inclusive and specialist settings across education, health, social care and leisure. The two publications form updated versions of *Including Me* (Carlin 2005) and *Dignity of Risk* (Lenehan and others 2004). The main difference between these two publications is the group of disabled children covered by each.

*Making it work for children with complex health care needs* focuses on children who require clinical procedures, children who require moving and handling and children who need intimate care as part of their personal support.

*Making it work for children with behaviour that challenges* focuses on those children who have behaviour that is challenging as a result of either a severe learning disability and/or autism.

## Define the children

> "Challenging behaviour is defined as culturally abnormal behaviour of such an intensity, frequency or duration that the physical safety of the person or others is likely to be placed in serious jeopardy, or behaviour that is likely to seriously limit use of, or result in the person being denied access to, ordinary community facilities."

(Emerson 1995, p.4 – 5)

Challenging behaviour is behaviour that others find 'difficult' or a 'problem'. Put another way, it is behaviour that challenges us as adults and as communities to find better ways of supporting a child or young person who is displaying 'difficult' behaviour.

> "Difficult behaviours are 'messages' which can tell us important things about a person and the quality of his or her life."

(Pitonyak 2005, p.2)

It can be but is not necessarily a diagnosis in its own right but rather a description of types of behaviour. Within the context of this publication, the term has been specifically applied to children[1] who have severe learning disabilities and/or autism, although the term is used in relation to other children and young people. Information on how autism can affect learning and behaviour is summarised at the end of this chapter.

The term challenging behaviour was developed to describe very difficult behaviour and to try to change perceptions about the behaviour being identified as the individual's 'problem'. It aims to conceptualise the behaviour as being a *challenge to others* – and therefore *the responsibility of others* to understand, change, adapt and find solutions.

Challenging behaviour is any form of behaviour that:

- interferes with a child's learning or development
- is harmful to the child, other children or adults.

Challenging behaviour can take a variety of forms including:

- verbal or physical outbursts
- self-inflicted injury, such as head banging
- stereotypic behaviours such as obsession with routine or order
- disruptive behaviours such as shouting or laughing out loud at inappropriate times
- sensory behaviours – under or over-sensitivity to sensory stimuli
- destructive behaviours that cause damage.

An individual may display one of more of these types of behaviour, to varying degrees.

Service providers need to understand that these behaviours are not generally under the control of the individual child or young person and they should be viewed as their way of communicating that they have been presented with an environment they find challenging. It is very easy to misconstrue or misunderstand what a child or young person's behaviour is telling us but, on the other hand, interpreting the behaviour correctly results in services being much better equipped at supporting the child and thus providing a much better experience for both children and staff. Service providers should also have a flexible approach as to what constitutes challenging behaviour within a particular situation or environment.

There is no simple explanation as to why challenging behaviour occurs, but because the social and communication skills of children with severe learning disability and/or autism are generally impaired or delayed, some may develop challenging behaviour as a way of communicating their needs or trying to 'shut out' stimuli that they find difficult. As they grow up, they are exposed to some of the educational and social demands made on other children, but they may be less able to handle them. Early intervention for children displaying challenging

---

[1] For ease of reading the words child and children are used to refer to both children and young people throughout this document.

behaviour is therefore key, so that the impact of the behaviour can be minimised and managed positively.

The severity of challenging behaviour can vary greatly and in most instances the term is used to refer to behaviour that does not have immediate serious consequences but is, nonetheless, very upsetting, disruptive or stressful. What is important is for service providers to recognise that for this group of children and young people, all behaviour happens for a reason and serves a purpose for the child even if it appears to make no sense to others.

In order to successfully provide a service to this group of children and young people and ensure that it is a positive experience for them, service providers must therefore understand why a child is engaging in such behaviour, what that behaviour is communicating and what positive behaviour strategies can be used to manage it. This publication will detail the steps service providers can take to enable this to happen.

## Prevalence

The latest figures from the Office of Disability Issues (ODI) indicate that 9 per cent of the child population are regarded as disabled, using the definition of disability in the Equality Act 2010 (Office for National Statistics 2009). Within this group of children, a small percentage will fall within the remit of this publication.

Disabled children do not fit neatly into one category or another, nor are definitions of impairments or conditions sufficiently well defined that it is possible to provide precise details of the disabled children in the population who will fall within the remit of this book. However, we do know that the prevalence of children on the Autistic Spectrum has increased substantially over the past 20 years and therefore the population of children using services is radically different from 10 years ago. There is also a move towards ensuring that all disabled children, even those with the most severe and complex level of learning disability or challenging behaviour, are included in local services and activities.

The information available from research is as follows. Two recent research studies (Emerson and Hatton 2008a; 2008b) have given figures based on the information collected on special educational needs (SEN) of all children in maintained schools and non-maintained special schools. Of the 8.2 million pupils (in January 2006) 171,740 (2.1 per cent) had an identified primary SEN associated with moderate learning difficulty (MLD), 30,440 (0.4 per cent) had an identified primary SEN associated with severe learning difficulty (SLD) and 8,330 (0.1 per cent) had an identified primary SEN associated with profound and multiple learning difficulty (PMLD) (Emerson and Hatton 2008a). They state that this is likely to be an underestimate and does not include pre-school age children. Using the 2008 School Census (Emerson and Hatton 2008b) the estimates per 1,000 children were:

- 35.8 for MLD
- 4.63 for SLD
- 1.14 for PMLD
- 8.20 for ASD.

The National Autistic Society estimates that the prevalence rate for autism is around 1 in 100 children. The NICE Clinical Guidelines on autism in children published in September 2011 stated that recent studies (Baird and others 2006, Baron-Cohen and others 2009) have reported increased measured prevalence rates, so that the minimum prevalence of autism is now regarded as 1 per cent of the child population. The increase in numbers of children on the autistic spectrum in recent years cannot be attributed entirely to earlier and widened diagnosis but increased awareness has led to more children being diagnosed with severe learning disability. Approximately 50 per cent of children on the autistic spectrum also have learning disabilities (Emerson and Hatton 2008b). There has also been an increase in the numbers of very premature babies that survive with very complex needs.

## How autism might affect learning and behaviour

*(This next section has been written by Joy Beaney and Kay Al Ghani, Torfield Community School and Inclusion Service, Hastings)*

Children with autism often exhibit unusual aspects of thought and behaviour that may cause challenges for them and those who support them, particularly in mainstream services. However, some of these characteristics can be strengths and understanding these will help staff to offer a suitable approach to supporting them. Staff and carers need to understand the mindset of children with autism and then examine practice in the classroom or service setting to ensure that their needs are met.

Children and young people with autism have difficulties with social relationships. This may cause problems making and sustaining friendships. They often do not understand their peer group's rules or misunderstand others' behaviour. Research by Wittemeyer *et al.* (2011), which looked at outcomes for people on the autistic spectrum, noted that 'difficulties fully understanding or "getting" social situations often impacted on peer relationships. These difficulties may lead to depression or an increase in aggressive behaviour'.

As children reach the teenage years and peer acceptance becomes more important, children with autism may have difficulty 'fitting in'. This could result in the young person becoming a target for bullying and adults will need to be aware of those who are particularly at risk. Batten *et al.* (2006) found that over 40 per cent of children with autism have been bullied at school. It is important to explicitly teach social skills and behavioural expectations to children with autism.

Children with autism may have problems empathising. They often do not realise other people have ideas or thoughts that differ from their own. This can lead to a misunderstanding, as they do not see the need to explain a situation. The child may not pick up meaning from others' body language resulting in them not recognising the non-verbal clues showing that a person is getting angry or upset and therefore may not respond appropriately to the situation. This is often referred to as difficulties with 'theory of mind'. A neurotypical child will experience many feelings when they get into trouble. One of these is acute embarrassment, or a feeling of humiliation that can stay with them for many years, especially if they feel they have been dealt with unjustly. This uncomfortable feeling is usually enough to get them back on the straight and narrow, but the child with autism will have very different feelings. To feel humiliation and embarrassment you need to care what other people think of you, indeed, you need to know what other people think of you. The difficulty with theory of mind, encountered by children on the spectrum, means this is not something that they understand instinctively. They also may find eye contact difficult and this could result in them being thought of as rude.

Children with autism are often preoccupied with parts of an object rather than the whole. This is sometimes referred to as central coherence deficit and can result in the child having difficulty connecting concepts and seeing the whole picture.

Sensory difficulties can be a major cause of behaviour problems. The child may be hypersensitive to a stimulus that does not worry us; for example, they may refuse to wear a certain item of clothing as it feels painful to them. Such hypersensitivity can relate to any of the senses such as noise, taste, smell or visual stimuli such as particular lights. Over-stimulation could stem from sensory overload. Anxiety can increase during the day and then the child loses control and can become upset, withdrawn or aggressive.

Some children with autism may have the opposite difficulty – hyposensitivity. Hyposensitivity is where children are 'under-sensitive' to stimuli and have trouble processing information through their senses.

A child with autism may be highly knowledgeable about something that interests them and will often talk for a long time about their special interest. These interests, however, can become obsessions and they may have difficulty focusing on anything else. Many people with autism have very good memories and are able to recite large chunks of information but this can mask a lack of understanding about a topic. Within the classroom, this can lead to misunderstandings and result in the child exhibiting challenging behaviour.

Children with autism have a need for routine and order. They often enjoy educational activities that are repetitive and which many students without autism would find 'boring'. However, new experiences or changes to routine can create uncertainty and lead to anxiety.

Children with autism create their own routines and it is often only if you interrupt or change how they do something that you realise how dependent they were on that pattern of events for security and understanding. Challenging behaviour may occur through the child having problems coping with the differing behavioural expectations of the many staff they encounter during the day.

## Partnership with parents and children

Providing services to children and young people whose behaviour challenges requires partnership working across a range of agencies and in particular a partnership with the child's parents, who in most cases will be the prime holders of key information. If children and young people with the additional needs outlined in this publication are to receive the very best support and a positive experience within services, there must be a two-way partnership between parents and staff. Chapter 5 gives detailed information about what services need to do and take into account in order to successfully work in partnership with parents.

Early Support is a way of working that aims to improve the delivery of services for disabled children, young people and their families. The Early Support Programme has produced a Multi Agency Planning and Improvement Tool, which is designed to inform and underpin service improvement for disabled children, young people and their families. It enables multi-agency groups, parent carers and young people to use the Early Support principles to review services, identify service development priorities, plan for improvement and track progress over time (www.ncb.org.uk/early-support).

# Checklist for inclusion

The following areas form a checklist for services to use to ensure that everything is in place in order to include disabled children in a way that is safe and balances the interests of the child, their parents, other children using the service and staff working in the service. These areas are explored in greater detail in Chapters 4 to 13:

1.  partnership arrangements, joint policies and protocols
2.  information on the child – working in partnership with parents and carers, including consent
3.  promoting a partnership with the child, including consent
4.  care plans
5.  positive behaviour support plans
6.  risk assessments for inclusion
7.  communication
8.  training
9.  written information
10. written records
11. review and monitoring.

Much of the above is equally applicable to disabled children who receive their services and support through **individual budgets and direct payments**.

An individual budget is where a family is given control over the funding allocated to them and can use it to develop their own package of support. Families can either take their individual budget as a direct payment or leave the council with the responsibility to buy the services on their behalf. Families can also choose to go with a combination of the two.

The arrangements for risk assessments to be carried out and support staff to be trained – where they are employed by the parents of the disabled child – must be as robust as those for directly provided services. When agreeing direct payments the issues of safety need to be taken into account by the local authority before agreeing a payment. It would not be acceptable in law for direct payments to be refused to disabled children who have behaviour that challenges on the grounds that a local area cannot put in place procedures that meet the necessary requirements.

# References used in this chapter

Baird, G, Simonoff, E, Pickles, A, Chandler, S, Loucas, T, Meldrum, D and Charman, T (2006) 'Prevalence of disorders of the autism spectrum in a population cohort of children in South Thames: the Special Needs and Autism Project (SNAP)', *Lancet*; 368: (9531)210 – 5.

Baron-Cohen S, Scott FJ, Allison, C, Williams, J, Bolton, P, Matthews, FE and Brayne, C (2009) 'Autism spectrum prevalence: a school-based U.K. population study'. *British Journal of Psychiatry*; 194: 500 – 9.

Batten, B, Corbett, C, Rosenblatt, M, Withers, L and Yuille, R (2006) *Make School Make Sense. Autism and Education: The Reality for Families Today*. London: The National Autistic Society. www.autism.org.uk/get-involved/campaign-for-change/learn-more/our-campaigns/past-campaigns/make-school-make-sense.aspx

Carlin, J (2005) *Including Me: Managing Complex Health Needs In Schools and Early Years Settings*. London: Council For Disabled Children.

Challenging Behaviour Foundation Website www.challengingbehaviour.org.uk

Emerson, E (1995) *Challenging Behaviour: Analysis and Intervention in People with Learning Difficulties*. Cambridge: University Press.

Emerson, E and Hatton, C (2008a) *People with Learning Disabilities in England*. CeDR Research Report 2008: 1.

Emerson, E and Hatton, C (2008b) *Estimating future need for adult social care services for people with learning disabilities in England*. CeDR Research Report 2008: 6.

Lenehan, C, Morrison, J and Stanley, J (2004) *The Dignity of Risk: A Practical Handbook for Professionals Working with Disabled Children and their Families*. London: Council for Disabled Children.

My Rights Your Responsibilities www.councilfordisabledchildren.org.uk/rightsresponsibility

National Autistic Society www.autism.org.uk/about-autism/myths-facts-and-statistics/statistics-how-many-people-have-autism-spectrum-disorders.aspx

National Institute for Health and Clinical Excellence Guidelines (2011) *Autism; recognition, referral and diagnosis of children and young people on the autism spectrum*. http://www.nice.org.uk/nicemedia/live/13572/56424/56424.pdf

Office for National Statistics (2009) Life Opportunities Survey: Interim Results, 2009/2010

Pitonyak, D. (2005) *10 Things You Can Do to Support A Person With Difficult Behaviors*. www.dimagine.com

Wittemeyer, K, Charman, T, Cusak, J, Gulberg, K, Hastings, R, Howlin, P, Macnab, N, Parsons, S, Pellicano, L, and Slonims, V (2011) *Educational Provision and Outcomes for People with Autism*. London: Autism Education Trust.

# 2. Balancing rights, benefits and risks – policy and legislation

## Introduction

In recent years, the UK has become much more concerned about risk. This is, at least in part, due to a culture of litigation and compensation. At the same time, the care and support needs of disabled children have become more challenging with an increase in the number of disabled children with high support needs, as described in the previous chapter. Services who are not experienced at meeting the needs of disabled children who have behaviour that is considered challenging worry that they will not be able to include them without an adverse impact on other children in the setting. This means that many disabled children find it difficult to access and join in a range of services across education, short breaks, play and leisure as they are considered too great a risk. Yet it is possible to include disabled children with the most complex of support needs providing services adopt a 'can do' attitude and manage risk effectively. It is also vital to consider the benefits to disabled children and their families of children being positively and appropriately included in settings and services.

## Effective risk management

"Services are good at highlighting the downside of risk – but poor at thinking about the great opportunities that facing up to risk and finding positive solutions in a creative and mindful way could mean for people, their families and their communities".

(Neill and others 2008)

Effective risk management requires service providers to give equal consideration to:

- the child's legal rights and entitlements;
- the risks, for both the child and the staff associated with including the child; and
- the benefits to both the child and their family of accessing a service.

This chapter looks at legislation and policy and outlines the need to find a balance between risk to the child, other children and staff and the rights and entitlements of the child to access services.

# Risk

Service providers have a duty to ensure that disabled children are not exposed to unacceptable risks and they are responsible for ensuring that their staff or carers are not being reckless or negligent when they provide a service. This duty can be met by an assessment of the potential risks and by avoiding those risks that are unnecessary. If the risk is necessary as part of a child's daily care, effective controls should be put in place to reduce the risk to a level which is 'reasonably practicable'. [2]

There will of course be instances where even providers with a 'can do' attitude cannot reduce the risk to a level that is reasonably practicable. For example, if a short break service places a child who has behaviour that is considered challenging and who requires moving and handling with a short break foster carer, consideration needs to be given to the fact that as the child becomes older and heavier and can no longer be carried upstairs by the carer, alternative arrangements may need to be found. For many services if the child stays with the carer one weekend a month the cost of equipment and adaptations to the carer's house would be regarded as unreasonable in relation to the amount of time that the child stays, or the house may be unsuitable for the appropriate equipment and adaptations. One would expect a service to explore the options creatively, taking into account that the child and carers have over time developed an important relationship. So, although an alternative placement may need to be found, the relationship between the child and the carers should continue.

Because children's support needs vary so widely, a risk assessment needs to be carried out for each individual child or young person, and for each of the services they receive, as potential hazards are likely to be different for each child in each setting. Although a checklist of potential hazards can be helpful, it can never be completely comprehensive so clear advice and guidance must be given to staff and carers on making the setting that the disabled child attends safe, and service providers must ensure that their carers can safely carry out their tasks, specific to the child's needs. This is essential both for the safety of the carer and the child. It is equally important that the health and safety of a child's own home is risk assessed if that is where the care is to be provided. A balance obviously has to be found between imposing health and safety requirements on a family and ensuring that an in-home carer, as well as the care she/he provides, is safe, both from their perspective and from the child's.

The Checklist for Inclusion detailed in this book provides a sound framework for assuring the safety of both carer and child.

---

[2] Reasonably practicable is defined by the Health and Safety Executive (HSE) as 'an employee has satisfied his/her duty if he/she can show that any further preventative steps would be grossly disproportionate to the further benefit which would accrue from their introduction' (HSE 1992, p.8)

# Health and safety responsibilities

Anyone who takes on a caring role (whether it is as an employee, an individual in a self-employed capacity or a foster carer) is subject to the common law principle of a 'duty of care', which requires that they preserve life, health and well-being. If an incident occurs whereby a child or young person is harmed or where a child or young person harms someone else while in the care of a service, then that service must be able to demonstrate that the incident was not as a result of the failure of a carer or staff member to carry out the responsibilities and duties laid out in the risk assessment and care plan for that child. The service must also be able to show that the risk was assessed and managed correctly. If they cannot demonstrate that they had taken reasonable steps to avoid that incident, there are in law two charges that could be brought against them:

1. Negligence – where staff failed to do something it was their duty to do and a foreseeable loss happened as a result.

2. Recklessness – where staff knew there was a risk, but either did not manage that risk or knowingly allowed the situation to occur in spite of the risk.

In either of these two charges, staff cannot claim that they were unaware of the risk. They must be able to demonstrate that they assessed all relevant areas of risk and that they took adequate steps to minimise it.

## Concerns

During the 1990s, services expressed **five main concerns** about the inclusion of disabled children who have additional support needs, including behaviour that challenges (Lenehan and others 2004):

1 **Fear of liability or litigation.** Staff feared they would be blamed if something went wrong and the child injured themselves, or another child, using the service or injured a member of staff. They did not feel they were in a supportive environment where the inclusion of children with behaviour that challenges was seen as positive.

2 **Lack of insurance.** Staff were not confident they would be adequately insured for providing a service to children who have behaviour that challenges if an injury or damage should occur. Insurance companies often viewed these children as 'too risky' and the rise of a compensation culture, together with the loss of Crown Immunity for NHS staff, compounded worries.

3 **Lack of training.** Staff in social care and education settings did not feel adequately trained to provide a service to children who have behaviour that challenges, and therefore felt unable to accept them in their services.

4 **Cost.** Services that would consider accepting children who have behaviour that challenges would often only do so with a 2 to 1 and sometimes a 3 to 1 staff ratio. This high level of staff support made the cost of provision expensive. In an environment where funding was limited, arguments about who should bear the costs of additional staff support and training remained central to decisions about service provision. The situation was further complicated by changing

definitions of health and social care as well an overall lack of agreement on joint funding, often exacerbated by local authority and health boundary issues. There was a clear need for joint agreement on the management of risk, backed by joint protocols and joint financing.

5 **Direction and advice.** Staff working in services were uncertain and confused about how to effectively manage a child's behaviour. The limited awareness of positive behaviour strategies and the lack of clarity on sanctions that could be used meant that many services considered some children too challenging to be included, even in specialist service provision.

# Rights of Access

## The United Nations Conventions

The right or entitlement to access services is underpinned by two UN Conventions:

- The UN Convention on the Rights of the Child (1989) was ratified by the UK in 1991. This convention states that all children, regardless of their race, disability or gender have the right:

  - not to be discriminated against
  - to have their best interest taken into account
  - to participate in decisions about their lives

- The UN Convention on the Rights of Persons with Disabilities (UNCRDP) (2006) was ratified by the UK in 2009. The Convention states that disabled people have the same rights as everyone else to freedom, respect, equality and dignity. Article 7 within this Convention also recognises the rights of disabled children and young people, but crucially goes further by specifically recognising that disabled children and young people should have 'full enjoyment of all human rights and fundamental freedoms on an equal basis with other children'.

Article 19 recognises that disabled people have the right to live and participate in the community with section C stating that countries that have adopted the Convention should ensure that 'services and facilities for the general population are available on an equal basis to persons with disabilities and are responsive to their needs'. Article 30 recognises the right of disabled people to take part on an equal basis with others in cultural life.

# Legislation and judgements

The right of disabled children to access services has been laid out by a number of laws, policies and judgements. Probably the two most important are:

- The East Sussex Judgement 2003
- The Equality Act 2010.

## The East Sussex Judgement 2003

Prior to the East Sussex Judgement in 2003, many services were 'managing' risk by totalling eliminating it, in other words they were not providing services to disabled children or adults whom they considered too risky. Unfortunately, this can still be the case even today and so it is crucial that all service providers understand the importance and relevance of this judgement in managing the rights/risk balance.

The legal case concerned a challenge to the 'no lift policy' adopted by East Sussex who had introduced a blanket ban on care workers manually lifting any disabled child, adult or elderly person because of the risk to care workers. The case focused on two young women, sisters living at home with their parents, where the local authority insisted that hoists were used to lift them. However, this method caused them considerable pain and their request to be lifted manually was refused, resulting in their care package breaking down and leaving their parents unsupported.

The significance of the judgement in this case is that it made 'no lift' policies illegal. The judge emphasised the need for a balanced approach to the rights of the disabled person and the rights of workers to be protected by health and safety regulations. She ruled that the imposing of a blanket ban on manual lifts represented a no risk regime or a risk elimination regime rather than one that seeks to offer independence and dignity to disabled people while minimising risk to workers. The judgement further clarifies that disabled people have the right to participate in community life, and that access to recreational activities is so important that a significant amount of manual handling might be required. It also makes clear that there may be some instances where lifting a disabled child or adult may not be 'reasonably practicable' but that decision should not be made without a thorough risk assessment that takes into account the impact on the disabled person, their wishes, their feelings and their human rights.

## The Equality Act 2010

The Equality Act 2010 provides the legal framework that protects disabled children from discrimination and promotes equality of opportunity. The Equality Act replaced all the pre-existing equality law on disability, race and sex discrimination and extends protection to new groups of people who share what are called *protected characteristics*[3]. The Act applies across most aspects of our national life, including the provision of services, education, transport, housing, and across the private, public and voluntary sectors.

The Equality Act replaced all earlier legislation on disability discrimination including the Disability Discrimination Act 1995, the disability sections of the Special Educational Needs and Disability Act 2001, and the Disability Discrimination Act 2005. The structure of the disability duties has changed, largely because of consolidation with duties owed to other groups of people who share protected characteristics, but the practical effect of the Act is broadly similar to that of earlier legislation and the definition of disability remains the same.

---

[3] Disability is one of the protected characteristics.

In the Equality Act different forms of discrimination are defined as *prohibited conduct.* These cover:

- treating a person (a child or an adult) less favourably than someone else because they are disabled – this is known as **direct discrimination**

- putting in place a rule or way of doing things that puts a disabled person at a disadvantage compared with someone who is not disabled, when this cannot be justified – this is known as **indirect discrimination**

- **harassment** – conduct that violates someone's dignity or which is hostile, degrading, humiliating or offensive to someone with a disability

- **victimisation** – treating someone unfavourably because they have taken (or might be taking) action under the Equality Act or supporting somebody who is doing so.

Two forms of prohibited conduct only apply to disabled people:

- treating a disabled person unfavourably because of something arising from their disability, when this cannot be justified – this is known as discrimination arising from disability

- failing to take reasonable steps to avoid putting a disabled person at a substantial disadvantage – this is usually known as the reasonable adjustments duty. This duty is anticipatory: it requires service providers to think ahead and make adjustments so that disabled people can participate, be included and providers can avoid any disadvantage that might otherwise occur.

The reasonable adjustments duty applies slightly differently to service providers, to colleges and to schools. To avoid disadvantage, service providers and colleges are required to make reasonable adjustments in relation to three different aspects:

- to any provision, criterion or practice, that is, the way that the institution organises itself, deploys resources and the day-to-day practices that it follows, whether or not they are written down

- to make alterations to physical features

- to provide auxiliary aids and services.

The reasonable adjustments duty applies differently to schools in that schools are not required to make alterations to physical features as part of the duty. The other two elements in the reasonable adjustments duty do apply to schools, see above.

Schools are however required to publish, resource and implement an 'accessibility plan'. An accessibility plan is a plan that sets out how, over time, the school is going to:

- increase access to the curriculum for disabled pupils;

- improve the physical environment of the school to increase access for disabled pupils; and

- make written information more accessible to disabled pupils by providing information in a range of different ways.

The Equality Act also protects people from being discriminated against:

- because they are associated with someone who has a disability – this includes the parent of a disabled child or an adult or someone else who is caring for a disabled person

- by someone who wrongly perceives them to have a disability.

A claim of disability discrimination against a service or a college is heard in the County Court. If a parent thinks that their child may have been discriminated against in school, they can make a claim of disability discrimination to the First-tier Tribunal (SEN and Disability), which is often known by its former acronym, SENDIST. A number of cases involving disabled children requiring medication have been taken to SENDIST and schools have been found to have discriminated because they failed to make reasonable adjustments to include disabled children in the curriculum, at school and on school trips. (See the references/links at the end of this chapter for further details of these.)

The Public Sector Equality Duty is a general duty, under the Equality Act, that applies to public bodies including public services, schools and colleges. It requires them to have due regard to the need to:

- eliminate discrimination, harassment, victimisation and other *prohibited conduct*

- improve equality of opportunity

- foster good relations between different groups of people: those who share a *protected characteristic* and those who do not.

Sitting under this general requirement is a specific duty requiring named public bodies, including local authorities, schools and institutes of further and higher education, to publish information and objectives to show how they are complying with the general duty.

The Equality Act allows service providers, schools, colleges and others to take action that may involve treating one group more favourably where this is a proportionate way to help members of that group overcome a disadvantage or participate more fully, or in order to meet needs they have that are different from the population as a whole. This is called 'positive action'.

## Entitlements to services

The right or entitlement to access services is protected by a number of other pieces of legislation. The most important are:

- Chronically Sick and Disabled Persons Act 1970
- Children Act 1989
- Children Act 2004
- Child Care Act 2006
- Children and Young Person Act 2008
- Children and Families Act 2014.

## The Chronically Sick and Disabled Persons Act (CSDPA) 1970

This Act applies to children as well as adults and gives an entitlement to an assessment of need. Under the Act, local authorities are required to make arrangements for a number of social care services if they are satisfied that it is necessary for them to do so in order to meet a disabled child or adult's needs. This may include practical assistance in the home, adaptations to the home and equipment, a sitting service, personal care, community-based services, help with transport and holidays. The Act was referred to in the 2009 Islington judgement concerning the use of eligibility criteria in disabled children's services when the judge ruled that local authorities can apply banding criteria to decide which groups of children they will consider to be eligible for services under Section 2 of the Chronically Sick and Disabled Persons Act.

## The Children Act 1989

The Children Act 1989 regards disabled children as 'children in need' requiring statutory services to safeguard and promote their welfare through the provision of a range of services and levels of support, appropriate to their needs. The kind of support and services provided should be designed to minimise the effects of disability and give disabled children and their families the opportunity to lead a life that is as normal as possible.

For the first time, the 1989 Act explicitly included disabled children in legislation that applies to all children. Previously services for disabled children were generally provided under disability legislation, which did not fully recognise the particular needs and legal status of children. The 1989 Act is an inclusive piece of legislation; disabled children are part of the wider group of children in need.

In the Wandsworth judgement ([2005] EWCA Civ 302) the court examined the relationship of the CSDPA and Part III of Children Act 1989 when arranging services for disabled children. The court said 'it shall be the duty of that authority to make those arrangements in the exercise of their functions under the said Part III'. Essentially this means services should be provided for disabled children under Part III of the 1989 Act, which gives the framework for children's services. Services have to be provided with an explicit focus on the needs of the child and the family. The 1989 Act imposes a coherent framework of child-centred requirements, which include most importantly the duties to safeguard and promote the welfare of children in need, and to find out and give due weight to the wishes and feelings of children and parents when providing services.

In all instances the decision to provide services follows an assessment of need.

"It is not, however, necessarily the case that services must be provided to meet every assessed need. Whether a children's services authority has to provide services following assessment is dependent upon the nature and extent of the need assessed and the consequences of not providing the service.
...the need can be met in a variety of ways".

(Broach and others 2010, p.79)

## The Children Act 2004

The ultimate purpose of the 2004 Children Act was to provide better protection for children of all ages. It included a duty on statutory and voluntary agencies to cooperate to promote the well-being of children. This is particularly beneficial to disabled children and young people who are more likely than other children to be known to a number of different agencies and whose inclusion in services and activities is dependent on the duty of these agencies to cooperate.

Rashid attends a youth club run by a national voluntary organisation. The staff need to be trained in moving and handling in order for Rashid to enjoy the activities offered by the youth club. The Children Act 2004 includes the duty on statutory agencies to work together with voluntary agencies so that children with additional needs like Rashid can benefit from the same services as other children. This would include support such as occupational therapy staff, from either social services or health, providing training for youth service staff.

## The Childcare Act 2006

The Childcare Act 2006, formalised the important strategic role local authorities play in childcare provision through a set of duties. These duties require authorities to:

- work with their NHS and Jobcentre Plus partners to improve the outcomes of all children up to five years of age and reduce inequalities between them

- secure sufficient childcare for working parents, paying particular attention to the need for provision of childcare that is suitable and accessible for disabled children

- provide a parental information service

- provide information, advice and training for childcare providers.

Maria is a single parent. Her son, Andrew, is three and has a recent diagnosis of autism. Maria would like to return to work. Under the Childcare Act 2006 the local authority, working with its health and employment partners, should be able to provide Maria with a list of affordable childcare providers who will care for Andrew and understand his support needs.

## Children and Young Persons Act 2008

Under section 25 of the Children and Young Persons Act 2008, local authorities have a duty to provide short breaks for disabled children and their families living in their area, the Short Breaks Duty. The overall purpose of the Short Breaks Duty is:

- to provide opportunities for disabled children and young people to enjoy themselves and fulfil their potential
- to enhance the abilities of parents/carers to care more effectively
- to enable families with disabled children to live an ordinary life.

The duties send a clear message that short breaks are not just for emergencies.

The legal requirements are as follows:

- Every local authority **must** provide breaks from caring for carers of disabled children.

- A range of short break services **must** be available.

- Every local authority **must** prepare and publish a short breaks services statement detailing the range of short breaks available and how disabled children and their families can access them.

- Every local authority **must** consult parent/carers in preparing the statement.

> Mark is 11 years old. He has a diagnosis of autism and behaviour that is described as challenging. His family have only been offered overnight residential short breaks as the local authority have no other short break services that they consider would manage his behaviour. Under the Short Breaks Duty, the local authority is required to extend the range of short break services so that Mark and his family are offered a choice of both specialist and inclusive mainstream services. Mark should, therefore, have a choice of either going to a residential unit or family-based carers for his overnight stays. He should be able to attend community-based activities, such as youth services or sports activities.

## The Children and Families Act 2014

Section 3 of the Children and Families Act sets out reforms to the special educational needs system.

The Act received Royal Assent in Spring 2014 and will be implemented from September 2014 onwards.

The Children and Families Act sets out a number of reforms to the rights and entitlements of children and young people with special educational needs and disabilities:

- Statements of SEN and Learning Difficulty Assessments (for 16 to 25 year olds) will be replaced by 'education, health and care plans' (EHC plans).

- The EHC plan will extend legal protections to young people aged 16 – 25 while they are in further education, training or an apprenticeship. Sixteen to 17 year olds who become NEET (not in education, employment or training) will also be covered.

- Local authorities and clinical commissioning groups must make arrangements for jointly commissioning services for children with SEN/disability in their area.

- Health commissioning bodies will have a duty to provide the health services set out in a child or young person's EHC plan.

- Local authorities must produce information on the education, health and care services they expect to be available locally (the 'local offer').

- Parents or young people with EHC plans will have the right to ask for a personal budget for their support.

- A parent or young person will be required to consider mediation before they can appeal to the SEN Tribunal. The mediator must be independent of the local authority.

- Introduce a pilot scheme to give children the right to appeal if they are unhappy with the plans for their support.

- Governing bodies will have a duty to make arrangements to support pupils at school with medical conditions.

## Inspection and registration

Many of the services used by disabled children will be registered with one of the inspection agencies – either Ofsted or the Care Quality Commission (CQC). Each inspection agency has a set of standards.

Ofsted uses a number of different inspection frameworks for the different services and establishments that it inspects: schools, children's centres, colleges, independent schools, local authority services, and provision registered on the Ofsted early years and childcare registers.

Social care services are inspected against the National Minimum Standards (NMS): Fostering Standards, Children's Home Standards, and Domiciliary Care Standards. Full details on the registration requirements for different short break settings are in the *Statutory Guidance on how to safeguard and promote the welfare of disabled children using short breaks* (DCSF 2010).

The exception of registration with a single agency is outlined in the Registration of healthcare at children's homes (CQC and Ofsted 2012). If a clinical procedure must be performed by a registered healthcare professional and may not be delegated to a competent layperson (in accordance with the Royal College of Nursing guidance) the service must be registered with CQC as well as Ofsted. If the task can be carried out by a competent layperson, trained and supported by a healthcare professional then the service need register solely with Ofsted.

## References used in this chapter

Broach, S, Clements, L and Read, J (2010) *Disabled Children: A Legal Handbook.* London: Legal Action Group. http://www.councilfordisabledchildren.org.uk/resources/cdcs-resources/disabled-children-a-legal-handbook

Convention on the Rights of Persons with Disabilities (2006) http://www.un.org/disabilities/convention/conventionfull.shtml

CQC and Ofsted (2012) *Guidance: Registration of Healthcare at Children's Homes.* http://www.ofsted.gov.uk/resources/cqc-and-ofsted-guidance-registration-of-healthcare-childrens-homes

Department for Children, Schools and Families (2010) *Short Breaks: Statutory guidance on how to safeguard and promote the welfare of disabled children using short breaks* https://www.education.gov.uk/publications/eOrderingDownload/short%20breaks%20statutory%20guidance%20march%202010.pdf

Health and Safety Executive, Manual Handling Registrations 1992 (as amended): Guidance on Regulations

Islington Judgement (*R (JL) v Islington LBC* (2009) www.bailii.org/ew/cases/EWHC/Admin/2009/458.html

Lenehan, C, Morrison, J and Stanley, J (2004) *The Dignity of Risk: A Practical Handbook for Professionals Working with Disabled Children and their Families.* London: Council for Disabled Children.

Neill, M, Allen, J, Woodhead, N, Reid, S, Irwin, L and Sanderson, H (2008) *A Positive Approach to Risk Requires Person Centred Thinking.* www.thinklocalactpersonal.org.uk

Stobbs, P (2013) *Disabled children, schools and the Equality Act 2010: What teachers need to know and what schools need to do,* London: Council for Disabled Children.

Wandsworth Judgement ([2005] EWCA Civ 302) www.bailii.org/ew/cases/EWCA/Civ/2005/302.html

**Newspaper and website reports of cases heard by SEND (Special Educational Needs and Disability Tribunal):**

http://www.teachingexpertise.com/articles/excluded-six-year-old-diabetes-wins-school-apology-363

http://www.telegraph.co.uk/health/children_shealth/4224145/Type-1-diabetes-how-schools-are-failing-some-children.html

http://www.guardian.co.uk/education/2009/feb/17/diabetes-children

http://www.guardian.co.uk/education/2009/mar/24/school-trips-disability

# 3. Current practice

In the context of this chapter, the term 'inclusion' means disabled children who have challenging behaviour being able to access services and support across education, health and social care that they and their families want and need. These services may be either mainstream or specialist. Some children and young people who have autism, for example, may have a far more positive experience in a specialist service or in one that is tailored to their individual needs. While some children do want to attend mainstream schools or services and are happy doing so, many who have behaviour that challenges experience difficulty in being accepted into mainstream services.

'Inclusion' may take a number of forms and some examples of different types of service inclusion are described at the end of this chapter.

Having established in the previous chapter that disabled children have a right to be included in services and activities, this chapter will focus on the barriers that existed to prevent this happening and the progress that has been made to remove some of those barriers.

## Overcoming the barriers

Over the past 10 years progress has been made on a number of fronts and this has led to greater inclusion of disabled children who have behaviour that challenges in both mainstream and specialist services. Although there is still much progress to be made, there have been positive changes:

- at a legislative and policy level

- in the way we perceive the place of disabled children in our society

- in tackling some of the process and practical issues that previously had prevented inclusion.

## Guidance

Policy guidance is written to assist commissioners, managers and practitioners implement the law. Within the area of short break services, the statutory guidance *(Short Breaks: Statutory guidance on how to safeguard and promote the welfare of disabled children using short breaks)* makes specific mention of the process services that are required to be used in order to ensure that disabled children are included safely (Department for Children, Schools and Families 2010).

# The place of disabled children in society

Over the past 10 years we have seen a move, supported by legislation and policy towards inclusion in every avenue of the lives of disabled children – education, health services, leisure, early years and other support services. The National Service Framework for Children, Young People and Maternity Services (NSF) (Department of Health 2004) set national standards for the first time for children's health and social care to promote high quality, child-centred services. Standard 8 focused on disabled children and young people and those with complex health needs. Despite this legistative underpinning the recent Life Opportunities Survey (LOS) (DWP 2011) found that children with impairments are more likely to have experienced participation restrictions when accessing services such as education and leisure. The survey found that the most common cause of this restriction was the attitude of others.

There are, however, a number of examples that illustrate a positive move towards a more inclusive society. One is the Aiming High for Disabled Children Short Break Transformation Programme introduced in 2007.

The government made a significant amount of money available to local areas over a three year period in order to transform short break services – services that parents had told them were the most important support to them in bringing up their disabled children. The programme specifically required local areas to look at ways in which disabled children could be included in universal provision wherever possible. The guidance stated:

"The Government believes that universal services should be the starting point when thinking strategically about how disabled children and young people can access positive experiences independently of their families."

(DCSF and DH 2008, p.10)

Evaluation of the effectiveness of this showed that a mixed economy of provision had developed:

"Inclusion and ordinariness. The increased use of community settings for short breaks has led to children and families feeling more included in society. However, many short breaks in inclusive settings are still segregated in how they happen. Both this more limited inclusion and other fully inclusive opportunities were driven by what parents wanted. Some parents wanted full inclusion – others did not."

(NDTi 2011, p.1)

When looking at opportunities what is important is that young people and their parents are given a genuine choice and a range of options from fully inclusive to specialist segregated provision across health, education and social care.

## Process and practical issues

**Joint working, integrated services** is an area where good practice is still variable and one of the barriers that remain to the inclusion of this group of children in service provision. There is no clear pathway as to how disabled children who have behaviour that challenges are supported to access either mainstream or specialist services and whether education, health or social care is the lead agency varies around the country. Some areas now have specialist autism teams in education that support staff to include children with autism in mainstream schools. This knowledge and awareness can then be shared with other services the child may want to access.

A report from the Every Disabled Child Matters Campaign states that despite national policy at a local level 'families talked about being caught between different agencies when funding is shared and of the need for key worker services to help them negotiate a complex system' (2011, p.4).

There are areas of good practice. For example:

*In Halton, services have recently been restructured and a very robust Early Help and Support Service has been established. This sits under social care but has the same front door for all professionals from which families can seek advice, support and service provision. It is now the biggest division within the authority, delivering a whole range of early help services to the whole family, including disabled children and their families. The service has developed a continuum of support from advice and information through to intensive support for those regarded as 'troubled families' and those on the edge of care. It is a multi-agency arrangement managed by the Children's Trust Board with full sign-up from those agencies. Some posts are funded by health and some healthcare professionals are based in the service for some of their working week. Halton have maintained their Children's Centres and staff from the new service are generally based in them. There are plans to increase co-location and joint posts.*

*The London Borough of Enfield are in the process of rolling out a local offer for children under 6 years of age who have an autism diagnosis. This bespoke offer will eventually be incorporated into the wider Special Educational Needs and Disability (SEND) Local Offer. Due to the increasing numbers of children being diagnosed as autistic, parents and professionals agreed to prioritise the development of resources to support parents of children newly diagnosed. Parents and professionals are now using the learning from this process to support the production of the wider SEND Offer. The new resources are:*

continued

- *a multidisciplinary Autism Spectrum Resource Allocation Panel (ASRAP)*
- *Making A Positive Start for Autism (MAPS for Autism).*

*ASRAP aims to bring together practitioners from Health, Education, Social Care and Parent Support Services for the purpose of receiving referrals from the Social Communication Clinic of all children given an autism spectrum diagnosis, in order that the local offer can be communicated to these families.*

*MAPS for Autism – Enfield have also set up a rolling programme of parent-child groups. MAPS for Autism is a series of five sessions for children with autism and their parents/carers. They provide an opportunity for children with autism to learn and develop their skills, whilst their parents and carers meet with professionals to find out more about autism, what support is available in Enfield and some top tips to support behaviour, communication and interaction. The sessions are being rolled out through children's centres.*

A diagram illustrating the proposed autism pathway for parents of children in Enfield is given at the end of the chapter.

**Insurance and liability** were among the barriers highlighted above. During the 1990s, advice from insurance companies was always the same: carers and staff would be covered to support disabled children who have behaviour that challenges providing that all 'reasonable steps' had been taken, as is the case with any risk activity. What needed to be established was what the 'reasonable steps' were.

*Dignity of Risk* (2004) was written in part to establish and disseminate this process of 'reasonable steps' in relation to disabled children with high support needs in social care settings. The process has been further developed and is outlined in this publication as the Checklist for inclusion; areas that any service needs to consider in order for disabled children to be safely included in all settings and activities.

**Training** is an area of practice where considerable progress has been made over the past 10 years in relation to the level and content of training required by staff and carers who will support children who have behaviour that challenges. In the absence of statutory guidance or any mandatory regulation of training, BILD developed the BILD Code of Practice (BILD 2001, 2006, 2010) for the use and reduction of restrictive physical interventions. This guide for trainers and commissioners of staff was first published in 2001 in response to an identified need to clarify standards relating to the training of physical interventions. This was with particular reference to services for children, young people and adults who have a learning disability or autism.

The following year the Department of Health and Department for Education and Skills published jointly *Guidance for Restrictive Physical Interventions* (DH, DfES, 2002).[4] BILD established the Physical Interventions Accreditation Scheme,

---

[4] This guidance is currently being updated.

based on the code of practice, national policy and legislation including the joint guidance. Organisations are accredited based on submitting evidence that their training satisfies each criterion of the code of practice. The 2006 edition included clarification of how the code of practice could be interpreted within mainstream school settings; this was viewed as a very positive addition.

The third edition of the code of practice was published in 2010 and continues to incorporate the most up-to-date policy and legislative developments in relation to both training and individuals for whom the training is intended. With each revision of the code more emphasis is placed on the inclusion of an appropriate values and attitudes base within training, one that sets out a positive approach to behaviour support and is fundamentally based on a person-centred assessment of individual risk.

The inclusion of physical interventions or restraint in training needs to be based on the risk assessment and considered only as a last resort and any intervention used needs to be proportionate and appropriate to the risks presented. The principles of the code and the accreditation scheme endeavour to maintain appropriate professional relationships and boundaries, accepting that people will normally be using the code in services in which they have identified the levels of risk and know the people they work with and support well.

Previously, staff would be equipped with a list of prohibited sanctions and very little advice, guidance or training on positive behaviour strategies, communication, and prevention and de-escalation skills. Training now focuses on physical restraint as a last resort, not as a method of 'controlling' behaviour. There has also been an increased awareness of the important role that parents should play in training support staff to understand and manage their child's communication and behaviour. BILD continues to run the accreditation course for training delivered across a wide range of children and adults health, social care and education settings.

References for two publications that give clear guidance for services developing policies on restrictive physical interventions are included at the end of this chapter. They include examples of good and poor practice and checklists to assist implementation.

**Direction and advice** given to staff and carers is now much clearer as a result of the changes that have taken place and better awareness of behaviour management. In the past, physical restraint ('reasonable force') was used to manage and control behaviour. There has also been a growing awareness that mechanical restraint should only be considered as a last resort and when no other option has been effective. Other interventions should always be explored as once the mechanical restraint is removed the behaviour is likely to return unless other strategies have been introduced or the cause of distress removed.

Unfortunately, there is still too reactive an approach to 'behaviour' and this book seeks to ensure that staff working with children understand behaviour as part of a child's method of communication, and an extremely important one if their ability to communicate verbally is limited. So, rather than keeping a child isolated to avoid them reacting to difficult situations, staff could explore adaptations to make these situations less challenging.

We have moved away from 'no contact' policies that led to situations where, for example, a young child who had fallen over could not be touched and comforted, or where a child with no concept of danger was allowed to run into the road as control was prohibited. Fortunately, there is now a more balanced approach to physical contact and updated guidance issued soon. A link to the updated guidance will be on the CDC website once it is final.

We have also moved away from a heavy sanction based system to the greater use of rewards. There is now a more balanced approach that acknowledges that the child's behaviour is their way of communicating a need. Currently many settings are using positive behaviour management strategies instead of focusing on sanctions to change behaviour.

Features of this good practice include these proactive strategies:

- **Adapting the physical environment.** The following extract from a leaflet produced for early years workers in Coventry identifies strategies for adapting the physical environment for children with autism:

    - Give instructions using clear, simple language and use visual reminders such as an object or picture to hold the child's focus on what has been said.
    - Use a quiet signal such as wiggling your fingers in the air to get a child's attention.
    - Stand or sit with your back to a wall rather than a window when you talk.
    - Create defined areas for different types of activity. If this is not possible think of a visual cue to help the child understand changes, for example, use a table cloth to change a writing table to a snack table.
    - Warn children in advance about loud noises if you can.
    - Create an area that is calm and quiet where children can go to relax. If you use screens or drapes to define the area, avoid bright colour and decorations that can be visually distracting.
    - Have an MP3 player with headphones so that children can listen to stories and music without being distracted by environmental sounds.
    - Have a box of objects that the child likes and which you can use to distract or calm him if he appears to be anxious.
    - Introduce new experiences, activities and resources gradually and sensitively. Include something that the child enjoys as part of the new experience.
    - Help children to focus on one idea at a time by minimising unrelated sensory stimuli.
    - Make sure that lighting is not too bright or harsh.
    - Eliminate sounds such as a rattling window or humming heater.

- **Providing consistency.** Use the same staff or carers to support children and young people, use the same behaviour strategies across agencies and services that the child accesses, maintain routines that are important to a child or young person across agencies and services that the child accesses where appropriate.

- **Providing visual support.** Provide support within the environment to aid understanding of routines and instructions. This can be done through the use of real objects/objects of reference, using photographs or other visual symbols or using simple signs or gestures. There are a range of symbols and symbol systems available, such as Boardmaker, Makaton and Widgit symbols (see Chapter 9 on Communication), which can be used to label objects, areas or routines as well as used in visual timetables to aid children's understanding.

- **Providing alternative and augmentative forms of communication (AAC).** To aid understanding and to enable methods of communication other than or in addition to verbal means of communication. Signing systems such as Signalong or Makaton can aid and support communication for children and young people. There are also systems of communication using symbols, such as PECS (Picture Exchange Communication System), which uses picture exchange. Symbols such as Boardmaker and Widgit can be used in both low and high tech communication aids to support communication. Applications for tablets and smartphones such as Proloquo2go are also becoming increasingly important and enable children to talk using symbols or typed text in a natural-sounding voice that suits their age and character.

**Boardmaker**

PECS

Widgit symbols

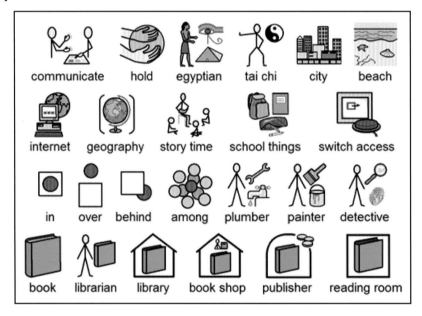

- **Anticipating and avoiding difficult areas/events if possible.** Knowing individual children is key to avoiding situations they may find difficult or may spark off challenging behaviours. A good way to ensure detailed knowledge of children is to ensure all children and young people have a simple 'personal communication passport' (see Chapter 9 for more details). Some general good practice strategies include, for example: allowing children and young people to have familiar possessions around them; giving the child plenty of personal space; not towering over the child – going to same level; and giving children plenty of time to respond to new situations or instructions.

Familiar routines with visual timetables and using simple language are a good way to ensure children feel settled. Be aware that when stressed, some children might withdraw (for example, put their fingers in their ears, close their eyes) while others might 'stim' (in other words, make motions such as flapping hands, rocking or flicking fingers in order to stimulate sensation or to deal with stress). This kind of behaviour may be calming to the individual so should not be stopped unless absolutely essential.

- **Using motivators.** Be aware of what the child or young person likes or enjoys and use these as rewards rather than withdrawing them as punishment; give an extra few minutes and praise for everyday tasks to help them understand what is happening around them, for example "that was good, well done" (for putting on socks). It is also useful to praise specific behaviour so that children and young people know exactly what they are doing well – for example, 'good waiting', 'nice colours'.

- **Teaching social skills.** Children with autism often have little social awareness. They may have no tact and might say exactly what they are thinking! People often find this very difficult to accept and they need to be made aware of the child's support needs so that they can understand and make allowances. This is an area where adults can give guidance and support and work with the child on acceptable and appropriate comments. Children with autism may misunderstand the intentions of other children or misinterpret social situations, which can cause challenging behaviour. It is often helpful to 'spell out' such situations clearly. Social skills, which children without autism generally pick up automatically, will need to be explained and taught to children with autism. Ongoing social skills groups would be of great benefit for many children with autism as a forum in which to discuss and learn new social skills and explore more acceptable outcomes to negative behaviour.

- **Sensory difficulties.** If the brain does not effectively process information from our senses and does not organise the information coming into the brain children may display unusual reactions to sensory stimuli. Many children with autism may be overly sensitive to certain sensations (hypersensitive), as a result of too much stimulation reaching the brain, or have low sensitivity (hyposensitive) where too little stimulation reaches the brain. Sensory difficulties can affect any of the senses. For example, hypersensitivity can result in touch being painful so that the child may react violently if someone brushes past them. A child may cover their ears and scream in response to the sound of a hand dryer if they are hypersensitive to sound. Smells can be intensified and become overpowering. The child may have difficulty tolerating movement and they may be frightened of activities where their feet leave the ground.

All these examples of sensory difficulties can easily lead to sensory overload. This can cause different reactions and behaviours that challenge, the child may 'shut down' and try to block out the stimulus, try to escape from the situation or become verbally or physically aggressive. Specialist Occupational Therapists can provide advice and support in identifying which sensory information can be challenging and when. Falkirk Council have produced a helpful booklet 'Making Sense of Sensory Behaviour', which would enable parents or settings to do so for themselves.

- **Encouraging communication.** It's most useful to know how much children understand and the way in which they communicate. In this way, you can pitch your own communication at the right level, which is the best way to enable understanding as well as encourage communication from the child. Generally speaking, don't always expect answers from the child; keep language simple and clear, one subject at a time; use direct requests such as 'stand up, please' rather than 'can you stand up?' A question to which the child may just respond 'yes!' In directing their actions, tell the child what you want them to do as it is easier for a child to do something than to stop doing something, for example, 'walk please' rather than 'stop running'. Use simple signs, gestures, symbols or pictures to support understanding if helpful.

Use simple descriptive praise so that the child can make a connection between their own actions and specific words of praise; keep communication simple and direct – no jokes, colloquialisms, sayings or sarcasm; use a calm, even and soft tone of voice; use non-verbal communication carefully; find out if the child has special words or signs for certain things – yes, no, food, toilet, more; or whether they use symbols to communicate.

- **Thinking about sleep.** There is a growing awareness of the consequences of poor sleep and sleep deprivation, not only for the individual but also for the impact it has on the whole family. This also affects daytime activity and the ability to function fully. However, there is not necessarily a universal understanding or tolerance of children and young people who have not had sufficient sleep. Whilst 40 percent of children have a sleep problem at some time in their development up to 86 percent of children with special educational needs are likely to suffer from disturbed sleep patterns at some point (The Children's Sleep Charity).

  Sleep problems can be divided into two main groups: settling problems, where the child has difficulty going to sleep at the appropriate time, and waking problems, where the child wakes repeatedly during the night and cannot self-settle. It is also important to remember that puberty can exacerbate sleep problems, as can excessively late bedtimes.

  Children and young people with a range of impairments are additionally disabled where their sleep is not sound. It is always worthwhile trying to remove sleep problems that may or may not be related to a disability but can be a source of great stress for the family. Continuity carers and short break providers should replicate family routines that work.

  Causes of poor sleep are varied but include light and noise pollution, poor routines and discomfort relating to a disability.

  Poor sleep leads to a greater likelihood of:

  - mood swings
  - anxiety
  - obesity and associated risks to the heart
  - diabetes
  - a greater risk of having an accident
  - poor functioning
  - less academic success or poorer cognitive development.

  It can also lead to poorer concentration, hyperactivity, behaviour that challenges and general irritability.

It's a good idea to encourage parents to keep a sleep diary so that they can keep a track of their child's sleep and identify any unusual patterns, or simply in order that they can evidence what is happening; a sample of a sleep diary is included at the end of this chapter.

A number of child development centres and Child and Adolescent Mental Health Services offer support to families around sleep issues where children have challenging behaviour.

The Children's Sleep Charity (www.childrenssleepcharity.org.uk) and Sleep Scotland (www.sleepscotland.org.uk) provide support to families around sleep issues. Sleep Scotland is based in Edinburgh but also works in England.

The Sleep Scotland website has a section relating to areas of the National Curriculum where opportunities exist to raise awareness of the importance of sleep. These are curriculum specific for England, Scotland, Wales and Northern Ireland.

Both charities run courses and work with families individually.

## Conclusion

Although many families and services, particularly in the voluntary sector, still feel like they are having to 'fight' the system in order for children to be included in both specialist and universal services, progress has been made in the past 10 years in overcoming some of the barriers that were identified in *Dignity of Risk* (2004). However, there are some children who are still considered 'too risky' for even specialist disability services. The purpose of this book is to assist services to consider in a systematic way the elements that need to be in place in order to ensure the effective inclusion of disabled children who have behaviour that is considered challenging.

> **Example 1:**
> **Specialist support within a mainstream secondary school**
>
> Stopsley High School in Luton has a place called 'The Hub', a name chosen by pupils and staff. This is a part of the school that children on the autistic spectrum, who have 'The Hub' provision included in their statement, can access at the times they need to, such as break times, lunchtime, or changing for PE. It provides a safety net that enables autistic young people to cope with the size and noise of a large mainstream secondary school. Although all school staff are autism aware, those based in 'The Hub' are particularly skilled and experienced. The young people who access the provision attend all mainstream lessons, but 'The Hub' is there if they are struggling or need additional support with a particular lesson.

## Example 2:
## Support to be included in a mainstream service

KIDS is a charity that provides a number of approaches and programmes for disabled children and young people. These include Home Learning (Portage), Parent Partnerships, Adventure Playgrounds and the inclusion of disabled children in mainstream settings. Their non-residential Short Breaks services provide opportunities where KIDS workers take the child or young person out into a community setting enabling them to have a positive experience while also giving their families a short break.

Hi, I'm Joe, I am 8 years old and I was born with no hands and I have learning difficulties. I live with my Mum and 2 brothers.

This is Mike, he is 19 and he is my Short Breaks Worker.

Mike visits me every week and we do all kinds of cool stuff. Most weeks I choose to go swimming.

We go by bus together to the swimming pool.

We have fun playing in the pool. Mike puts on my armbands and helps me to swim.

After swimming Mike helps me to get changed before we go home.

Mike is my friend, we do lots of fun things together.

I like the KIDS Short Break Service!

> **Example 3:**
> **Autism specific service**
>
> Brighton and Hove Children's Services commissioned the local Barnardo's short break service (Brighton and Hove Link Plus) to provide a contract carer scheme aimed specifically at children and young people with autism. Contract carers (also known as fee paid, salaried, professional or link-plus carers in some areas) are approved by a fostering panel as foster carers to provide short breaks on a 'full or part-time' basis. They receive a fee or 'retainer' throughout the year, even when they do not have a child staying. Additionally, they receive an allowance when a child is in placement, in the same ways as other short break carers. They are contracted to provide a specific number of nights per week or per year. The children are cared for in the homes of the carers both on an overnight and day care basis. Since setting up the scheme, Brighton and Hove Link Plus have recruited three part-time contract carers providing between 100 and 115 overnights per year and have successfully placed seven children on the autistic spectrum who stay with the carers from a few hours to between 40 and 60 overnights per year. The carers are highly skilled and have at least 2 years' experience of working with or supporting disabled children with autism and/or challenging behaviour. They have autism specific training and meet as a group of carers to share their experiences, ideas/suggestions to improve the service and provide support to one another.

# Book references

## *Physical Interventions: A Policy Framework*

John Harris, Marion Cornick, Alan Jefferson and Richard Mills

This book gives clear guidance for services developing policies on restrictive physical interventions. It includes examples of good and poor practice, checklists to assist implementation, an agenda for action at the end of each chapter and a summary of key policy principles. Chapter topics include the legal framework, risk assessment and employers' responsibilities.

The first edition became the key reference for anyone involved in working with adults and children who, because of their challenging behaviour, may need some kind of restrictive physical intervention. It has been revised to show how the four core principles identified in Valuing People (rights, independence, choice and inclusion) apply to the use of restrictive physical interventions. It also takes account of the widespread acceptance of person-centred approaches to service development, the introduction of the Mental Capacity Act 2005 and changes in terminology.

The book will be of particular interest to:

- providers and commissioners of adult and children's services
- schools and teachers of children with a learning disability or autism

- care staff, family carers and parents of children who present challenging behaviour
- OFSTED and CQC inspectors
- local education authorities
- clinical and educational psychologists
- psychiatrists working with adults and children with autism and learning disabilities
- learning disability and RNMH nurses
- dentists.

# Second volume

## *Ethical Approaches To Physical Interventions Vol II: Changing The Agenda*

Edited by David Allen

The topic of physical intervention is still hugely important: the abuse of such interventions features all too regularly in national scandals, and people with intellectual disabilities and others with complex needs are still dying in the UK as a result of the use of inappropriate restraint.

Through rigorous analysis of current policies and practices, careful examination of physical interventions and abusive practices, and clear discussion of objectives and needs for the future, this new publication offers a major overview of key developments and current best practice in the field.

Topics covered in the book are:

- the effectiveness of training in physical intervention
- reflections on accreditation
- evaluating the risks associated with physical interventions
- physical interventions and family carers
- mechanical restraint and self-injury in people with intellectual disabilities – an enduring cause for concern
- ethical use of medication to manage imminent disturbed/violent behaviour in adults with intellectual disabilities – Seclusion and time out? Questioning and defining practice
- restraint-related deaths: Lessons for policy and practice from tragedy?
- prevention is better than reaction
- getting our priorities right
- antecedent interventions for people with intellectual disabilities who present challenging behaviour
- teaching new skills to people with learning disabilities who engage in aggressive behaviour
- restraint reduction.

**Please note: this is a second volume to the Ethical Approaches series, not a second edition. It does not replace the first volume but complements it and updates the debate.**

## Making Sense of Sensory Behaviour: A Practical Approach at Home for Parents and Carers

Lesley Beath and Lindsay Park

This comprehensive leaflet is designed to help parents understand sensory issues which may drive their children's behaviour.

Reading the signs gives a wide-ranging list of sensory issues and behaviours that may be associated with them, which will help parents and carers or those working with children and young people identify which sensory information is being reacted to.

Advice/strategies for parents and carers covers:

- calming strategies if a young person is over-stimulated
- alerting strategies if a young person is not alert enough to pay attention to a task
- sensory strategies for personal care including dressing, personal hygiene, haircare and toileting
- calmer eating strategies
- general calming strategies.

The above includes both quick fixes to address a situation where a young person is over-stimulated and longer term strategies designed to help the young person feel calmer generally and therefore cope better.

The final section provides advice on how to identify and address possible sensory impacts on behaviour.

## Proposed Autism Pathway in Enfield

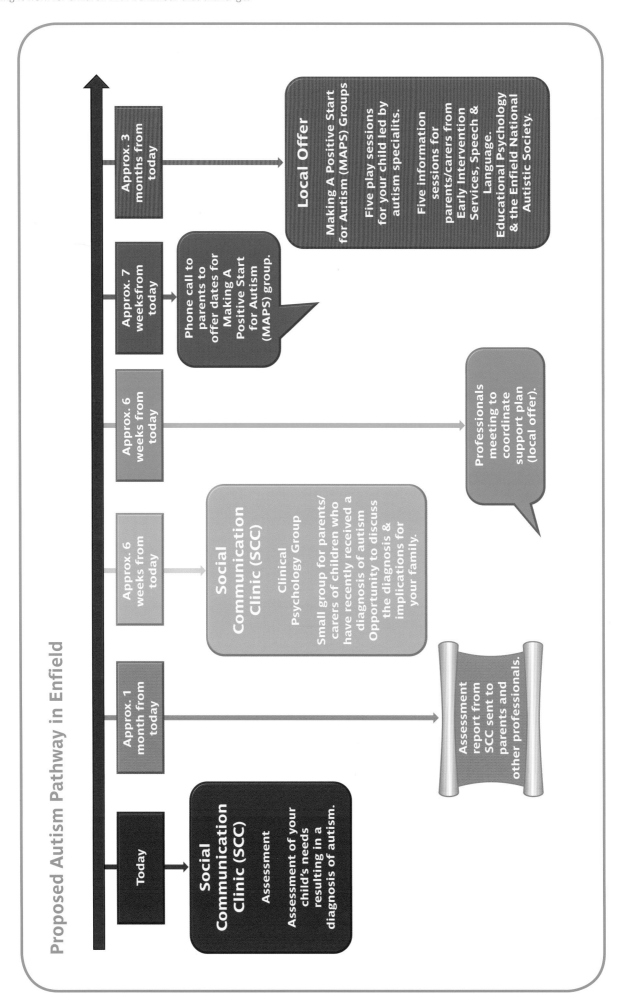

**Today**

**Social Communication Clinic (SCC)**

Assessment

Assessment of your child's needs resulting in a diagnosis of autism.

**Approx. 1 month from today**

Assessment report from SCC sent to parents and other professionals.

**Approx. 6 weeks from today**

**Social Communication Clinic (SCC)**

Clinical Psychology Group

Small group for parents/carers of children who have recently received a diagnosis of autism Opportunity to discuss the diagnosis & implications for your family.

**Approx. 6 weeks from today**

Professionals meeting to coordinate support plan (local offer).

**Approx. 7 weeks from today**

Phone call to parents to offer dates for Making A Positive Start for Autism (MAPS) group.

**Approx. 3 months from today**

**Local Offer**

Making A Positive Start for Autism (MAPS) Groups

Five play sessions for your child led by autism specialists.

Five information sessions for parents/carers from Early Intervention Services, Speech & Language, Educational Psychology & the Enfield National Autistic Society.

# Sleep Diary

Child's Name:          Date:          Child's DOB:

| | Day 1 | Day 2 | Day 3 | Day 4 | Day 5 | Day 6 | Day 7 |
|---|---|---|---|---|---|---|---|
| Any naps during the day? Please note time and duration | | | | | | | |
| Time bedtime routine started | | | | | | | |
| Time the child was in bed | | | | | | | |
| Did you stay or did they self settle? | | | | | | | |
| What time did they go to sleep at? | | | | | | | |
| Times they woke up in the night/ how long were they awake/ where did they go back to sleep? Your bed/their bed etc | | | | | | | |
| Time they woke up in the morning | | | | | | | |
| Total number of hours sleep | | | | | | | |

# The Sleep Cycle

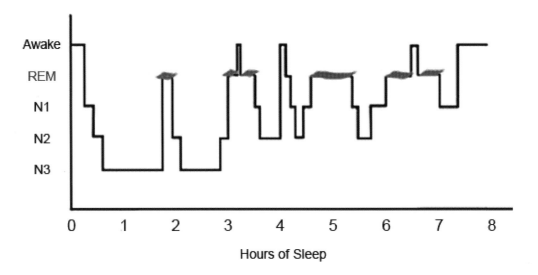

Hours of Sleep

Things that you need to know about your child's sleep cycle:

- Once they are 3 months of age each cycle lasts about 90 minutes

- Your child is most likely to awaken between cycles

- It takes about 10 minutes for children and older babies to fall into a deep sleep

- There are 2 types of sleep REM and non REM sleep

# References used in this chapter

Brett, J (2012) PowerPoint presentation for healthcare staff at Faculty for Health and Social Care. London: South Bank University.

The Children's Sleep Charity www.thechildrenssleepcharity.org.uk

Council for Disabled Children, written by Wheatley, H (2006) *Pathways to Success: Good Practice Guide for Children's Services in the Development Of Services for Disabled Children.*

Department for Children, Schools and Families (2008) *Aiming High for Disabled Children: Short Breaks Implementation Guidance.*

Department for Children, Schools and Families (2010) *Short Breaks: Statutory Guidance on How To Safeguard and Promote the Welfare of Disabled Children Using Short Breaks* https://www.education.gov.uk/publications/eOrderingDownload/short%20breaks%20 statutory%20guidance%20march%202010.pdf

Department for Children, Schools and Families, written by Murray, M and Osbourne, C (Children's Society) (2009) *Safeguarding Disabled Children: Practice Guidance.*

HM Treasury and Department for Children, Schools and Families (2007) *Aiming High for Disabled Children: Better Support For Families.*

http://www.ndti.org.uk/uploads/files/Insights_5_Short_Breaks_25_11_10.pdf
Lenehan, C, Morrison, J and Stanley, J (2004) *Dignity Of Risk: A Practical Handbook for Professionals Working with Disabled Children and their Families.* London: Council for Disabled Children and Shared Care Network.

NDTi (2011) *Short Breaks for Disabled Children and their Families.* Insights 5.

Department of Health (2004) *National Service Framework for Children, Young People and Maternity Services: Disabled Children and Young People and those with Complex Health Needs.*

Office of National Statistics and Department of Work and Pensions (2011) *Life Opportunities Survey, Wave 1.* https://www.gov.uk/government/uploads/system/uploads/ attachment_data/file/180896/children.pdf

Department of Health and Department for Children, Schools and Families (2008) *Aiming High for Disabled Children: Short Breaks Implementation Guidance.*

Every Disabled Child Matters and The Children's Trust Tadworth (2011) *Disabled Children and Health Reform: Questions, Challenges and Opportunities.*

BILD Code of Practice for the use and reduction of restrictive physical interventions (2001, 2006, 2010 editions)
www.bild.org.uk

Department of Health and Department for Education and Skills (2002) *Guidance for Restrictive Physical Interventions: How to provide safe services for people with Learning Disabilities and Autistic Spectrum Disorder.*

# 4. Partnership arrangements, joint policies and protocols

The provision of services to disabled children who have behaviour that is considered challenging cannot be achieved by any one agency or organisation working on its own. It is essential that agencies and organisations in any geographic area work together to create partnership arrangements so that all schools and settings in an area follow the same procedures and policies to ensure the inclusion of disabled children who have behaviour that challenges in all mainstream and specialist services.

The term 'challenging behaviour' can lead to difficulty in a child or young person accessing services and therefore their social exclusion. However, if agencies and organisations in an area work together, there will be greater clarity on how each service can include children who have behaviour that challenges by, for example, ensuring that their staff are properly trained and supported. Services should not be in the position of having to negotiate for funding to train staff each time a child with behaviour that is considered challenging wants to access their service. All areas should have joint policies and procedures in place that outline the process in that area.

Once a local area has an agreed arrangement in place each organisation or agency needs to incorporate this arrangement into the individual policies and procedures for their own organisation or service.

## Why is a partnership arrangement at an area level needed?

Wherever possible all agencies – health, social services, education and the voluntary or third sector – should come together to develop a jointly agreed policy and procedures detailing how disabled children who have behaviour that is considered challenging will be included in service provision.

Having a jointly agreed arrangement will:

- provide consistency of approach across an area and give status to that approach
- ensure the commitment of all agencies to providing shared governance and shared ownership of the process

- draw on the expertise and knowledge of staff in all agencies
- ensure that the roles and responsibilities of all agencies are clearly defined
- lessen confusion for parents about what tasks agencies and organisations can and cannot take on
- help to clarify the entitlement to a level of support that a child who has behaviour that is considered challenging may expect
- clarify the funding arrangements for support to the child.

# Who should be involved?

If possible all agencies – health, social services, education, voluntary or third sector – in your area should come together in a 'partnership group' and be involved in drawing up the policies and procedures. It is essential to involve parents of disabled children who have behaviour that is considered challenging or to be able to link into the local Parent Forums (a list of parent forums can be found at www.nnpcf.org.uk/regions). Although the 'partnership group' may, therefore, be a large group, once the basic outline for the policy is agreed most of the work can be done in smaller task groups.

Working in smaller groups will facilitate the ad hoc involvement of other specialists – for example, educational psychologists, clinical psychologists, SENCOs, speech and language therapists, behaviour support team, and so on – thus enabling the maximum sharing of knowledge and expertise across sectors and professional groups. It is vital to involve unions and professional organisations at an early stage of the development of the policies rather than consulting them at the end of the process. For example, if your policies are to cover inclusion in school it is essential to work with the local teaching unions and associations so that you have the backing of their members when it comes to implementation.

The policies and procedures may form part of a wider health and safety policy or include areas such as the giving of medication or the use of restrictive physical interventions. Each local area should develop policies and procedures that fit into the way partnership working takes place in that area.

The life of the 'partnership group' should not be limited to the development of the arrangements but should continue in order to monitor and update the arrangements.

# Monitoring and updating the policies and procedures

Once the local policies and procedures have been agreed they should be rolled out to organisations and agencies across the area, through a variety of means – training days, presentations and other one-off events. It is important to include service providers in the voluntary and third sector as well as parents in this roll-out so that they know what they can expect. It is also essential to find ways to ensure that governing bodies and management groups are aware of the policies – for example school governors, playgroup management committees, trustees of local charities etc.

*The following is an example from Halton who at the end of 2010 developed a service with health as a way of improving the quality of local services for disabled children, young people and adults who have behaviour that is considered challenging. Halton Borough Council, alongside St Helen's and Halton NHS, commissioned a specialist, peripatetic Positive Behaviour Support Service (PBSS). As well as improving quality, the new service was driven by a 'spend to save' philosophy as it was anticipated that the new service would lead to the avoidance or termination of high cost 'specialist' placements, often out of the area. Neighbouring authorities Knowsley and St Helens now also commission the service. Halton PBSS is the first Local Authority service in the UK to be staffed and led by Board Certified Behaviour Analysts (BCBA). It aims to work collaboratively in four related areas:*

- *early intervention*

- *crisis prevention and management*

- *technical support*

- *placement development.*

*Early Intervention work involves offering parent training workshops upon diagnosis, working with individual children, young people or adults and working closely with Education.*

*The prominent focus on crisis prevention and management involves developing competencies and mentoring staff in mainstream services, behaviour monitoring, the prevention of placement breakdown and out of borough placement and eligibility criteria for crisis situations. The service also aims to have a presence at key risk times, for example, transition from children to adult services, changes in staff, and placement changes such as moving school, attendance at a new day service, and so on.*

*In terms of technical support, the PBSS provides specialist individualised treatment for the most complex children and adults. This includes referral, review, and allocation for a full functional assessment, a person centred intervention plan and a clear service exit preparation and follow-up. Placement development involves returning children and adults who are currently out of borough to their local area and reviewing restricted in borough placements.*

*Since its establishment, the PBSS is going well and its 'four armed' pragmatic approach is proving successful. The quality of life for the individuals who have used the service has significantly improved and cost effectiveness has been clearly demonstrated. Halton's education service want to develop further joint working and service commissioners are keen to invest further.*

# Using Continuing Healthcare funding

Some areas will draw on Continuing Healthcare funding to support this group of disabled children. The National Framework for Children and Young People's Continuing Care (2010) involves a multi-agency funding process led by the NHS for children with such complex needs that they need services over and beyond what universal and specialist services can provide. The NHS leads an assessment process that takes into account the views of children and families, their assessed needs, as well as social care and education assessments. A multi-agency panel then decides whether additional services are required and how the agencies can work together to fund and provide them. This process is different from adult continuing healthcare where once eligibility is established the NHS pays for and commissions packages of support. The difference is an acknowledgement of the very different legislative and care needs of children. This can lead to difficulties at transition but both the children's continuing care framework and the adult continuing healthcare framework share the same transition process starting at 14, which is outlined in both the adult and children's framework documents.

# Adopting individual policy and procedures

The joint working arrangements in any area form the overarching umbrella under which each organisation or agency will write their own policy and procedures – appropriate to their organisation and the type of activities they run. An organisation's policy and procedures should be in line with the joint working arrangements in that area. For services that are part of national voluntary, third sector or private organisations the policies and procedures may need to be in line with both the local area arrangements as well as the policies of the national organisation. Where there are differences these will need to be resolved in the service level agreement or contract.

The policy and procedures covering disabled children who have behaviour that is considered challenging may be a standalone document or it may be part of an overall health and safety policy or inclusion policy. The document needs to be appropriate to the size and complexity of the organisation and the type of activities that are offered.

Having an individual policy will:

- demonstrate the commitment to positively including children who have behaviour that is considered challenging in service provision
- lead to a clear understanding of the roles and responsibilities of staff or carers
- clarify for parents and children what they can expect from a service and what is expected from them.

# What should a policy contain?

A policy should include information on:

- The roles and responsibilities of staff and carers with regard to supporting children who have behaviour that is considered challenging. In some settings, for example schools, the terms and conditions of employment of teachers do not include giving of medication or administering restrictive physical interventions. Schools therefore need to ensure that they have sufficient members of support staff who are employed and appropriately trained to administer medication, follow positive behaviour plans or carry out restrictive physical interventions, as part of their duties.

- Duty of care. Anyone caring for children has a common law duty of care to act like any reasonable responsible parent and make sure that children are healthy and safe.

- What the organisation expects from the parents in terms of being kept informed and updated about their child's behaviour, communication and medical needs.

- The training that staff and carers can expect to receive prior to supporting a child who has behaviour that is considered challenging. Staff or carers will need to be trained and supported by an appropriate professional or a BILD accredited trainer if restrictive physical interventions are likely to be used. The policy should outline the arrangements for the training of staff. Training is dealt with as a separate issue in Chapter 10.

- The ongoing support, monitoring and review of staff.

- Communication strategy; including policies and principles for supporting communication in children and young people and the links between communication and behaviour with appropriate strategies.

- Partnership working; to include links with parents and other professionals, enabling collaboration and joined-up approaches.

- Indemnity or insurance arrangements. All employers should make sure that their insurance arrangements provide full cover in respect of actions that could be taken by staff or carers in the course of their work. It is the employer's responsibility to ensure that proper procedures are in place and that staff are aware of the procedures and are fully trained.

- Staff may be anxious about taking on responsibility for supporting children who have behaviour that is considered challenging because they fear something 'going wrong'. In the event of a successful claim for alleged negligence it is the local authority or employer, not the employee who is held responsible and would meet the cost for damages, unless that member of staff has not followed their employer's policy. For example, the employer for an early years setting may be a manager or a management committee or for a voluntary organisation it will be the trustees of that organisation.

- Risk management, record keeping and protocols to be followed.

- Responses to emergency situations.

- Any additional arrangements that need to be in place for activities that take place away from the usual base or site.

> In order to ensure that the policy document does not remain unread on a shelf, the short breaks team in Coventry give each support worker a copy of their Health and Safety Information Pack and the worker signs to state that they have received a copy. The Pack covers information relating to their employment (time sheets and supervision); issuing of first aid kits; safety procedures for group activities, infection control, giving of medication, and risk assessments. The pack also contains the forms used for writing a short break plan, an outcomes plan, information on the child, as well as documenting the service or activity undertaken during the break.

## Supporting children who have behaviour that challenges and safeguarding

It is well established that disabled children are more vulnerable to all forms of abuse and the range of support that may be required increases this vulnerability. Additionally children and young people who display challenging behaviour are at risk of restrictive practices including:

- physical restraint
- seclusion
- mechanical restraint, for example arm splints.

While there may be occasions where a restrictive practice is necessary to keep a child or young person safe they should:

- be used as infrequently as possible
- be in the best interests of the child or young person
- be part of a wider Positive Behaviour Support plan (see Chapter 8)
- not cause injury
- maintain the child or young person's dignity
- be recorded and regularly reviewed.

Where these principles are not followed restrictive practices may be abusive. Further guidance is available from the Department of Health and Department for Education and Skills (2002) and BILD's code of practice (2010).

When agencies and organisations are writing policies and procedures they should link these to existing child protection policy at both an area and organisational level. Policies and procedures should make specific reference to the use of restrictive practices.

Sussex Community **NHS**
NHS Trust

## Intimate and Personal Care for Children and Young People

**Good Practice Guidance: Intimate Care**

Children and young people who require an adult to provide intimate care have physical, sensory and/or learning impairments, which influence their ability to carry out their intimate and personal care independently themselves. There is an increasing range of settings where the provision of safe and healthy intimate care needs to be delivered to ensure that all children whatever their abilities can be included in activities and opportunities throughout their childhood.

### What informs good practice in intimate care?

What we know from social, biological, psychological and developmental research and knowledge informs intimate and personal care practice which promotes child health, wellbeing and safety.

The adult supporting a child or young person with intimate care needs to consider both their *attitude and actions* within the approach.

### *Principal elements of safe and healthy intimate and personal care*

- *Trust and duty of care to safeguard the child*
- *A person centred approach*
- *Promoting the development of positive self esteem, body image and self confidence*
- *Promoting the development of appropriate relationships, sexuality and personal safety*
- *Integrating social and cultural values and beliefs*
- *Promoting positive lived experience and feelings of intimate care*
- *Promoting cleanliness and personal hygiene; preventing infection and disease*
- *Provision of education and training*

### Trust and duty of care to safeguard the child

The person designated to provide intimate and personal care to a child or young person is placed in a position of trust and has a duty through their responsibilities as a parent or as an employee to provide care which always promotes the health, wellbeing and safety of the child or young person. This includes protecting the child from abuse. Other family members are regarded as trusted adults and accordingly have a duty to safeguard the child or young person.

### Child Protection

Staff need to be aware that some adults may use intimate care procedures as an opportunity to abuse children and young people. Staff need to be aware of the possibility that allegations of abuse may be disclosed. Allegations can be made by children and young people and they can be made by other concerned adults. Allegations can be made for a variety of reasons. Some of the most common are:

- Abuse has actually taken place
- Something happens to a child that reminds them of an event that happened in the past – the child is unable to recognise that the situation and the people are different
- Children can misinterpret your language or your actions because they are reminded of something else
- Some children know how powerful an allegation can be; if they are angry with you about something they can make an allegation as a way of hitting out
- An allegation can be a way of seeking attention

**The following quality statements set out the best practice principles and guidance for staff and families.**

Quality Statements

1. Treat every child with dignity and respect and ensure privacy.

Intimate and personal care should be provided with dignity and respect ensuring privacy, this includes care being given gently and sensitively.

Adults should take into account the child's views and feelings throughout any procedure or intervention and give careful consideration to what the child is used to and what is appropriate, given their needs and their family's culture and beliefs. Information about a child/young person's intimate and personal care needs is both private and confidential. Information sharing relating to intimate care should be for a legitimate purpose and with the consent of the child/young person or where a child/young person lacks capacity the parent or guardian.

Privacy should be appropriate to the child's age, gender and situation. Privacy is an important issue. Children have a right to privacy and staff need to recognise that right and take steps to ensure it is upheld. It is important to ensure that e.g. changing clothes is done in a safe and respectful manner. Identified places for changing are therefore helpful.

Privacy can be respected by allocating one adult unless there is a sound reason for having more adults present. Where this is the case the reasons should be documented. Where two people are required for manual handling, staff should consider that once the initial manual handling task is complete, the second person could remove themselves until summoned once the intervention has finished and child has been re-clothed.

## Sussex Community **NHS**
NHS Trust

**2. Involve the child/young person in their own intimate care and be aware of and responsive to the child's reactions.**

The child should exercise choice as far as possible throughout. Staff should gain the child's consent or assent to carry out any procedure or intervention.

Any touch which is intended as 'help' (e.g. helping a child with toileting needs) is to be as enabling and empowering as possible and the child should be permitted to do as much by themselves as possible. Involve the child/young person as far as possible in their own intimate care and if the child or young person is able to help, give them every opportunity to do so. It is important to avoid doing things that the child or young person can do alone or with support. If a child is fully dependent on you, talk with them about what you are doing and give them choices wherever possible.

Children and young people should always be consulted about their views regarding touch and physical contact. Their understanding and acceptance of touch needs to be explicit. Staff and volunteers should check their practice by asking the child, particularly a child they have not previously cared for, e.g. 'Is it ok to do it this way?' 'Can you wash there or do this?'

Use your intuitive knowledge and experience of the child you are caring for and verbally report and document any changes in the child's behaviour or their reactions to intimate care.

**3. Encourage the child/young person to have a positive image of their own body.**

Providing intimate care with the right attitudinal approach with clear good practice actions provides ongoing opportunities to teach children about the value of their own bodies, develop self confidence and a positive self esteem. The approach adults take in providing intimate care to a child/young person should convey messages that their body and they are respected; a sense of value. Confident, assertive children/young people who feel their body belongs to them are less vulnerable to sexual abuse. Whilst keeping in mind the child/young person's age and understanding, routine care should be enjoyable, relaxed and fun.

Early years role modelling of good practice in intimate care experiences provides important personal safety learning for children. Understanding good touch/care behaviours throughout childhood enables the child to differentiate more easily when they experience abusive touch/care behaviours.

The gender of the adult care giver should take into account the child's age, developmental history, cultural beliefs and values and the expressed views of the child and/or parents and should be documented within the individual intimate care plan.

**Sussex Community NHS**

NHS Trust

As a general guide children up to the age of 8 can be provided intimate and personal care by either gender. From about 8 years of age as the child is developing their sexuality psychologically, physically and physiologically, the gender of the adult intimate care giver becomes more of an issue to the individual young person in terms of their respect for privacy, and their views and feelings are critical to deciding who should provide intimate care.

Where a young person lacks capacity to decision make the parent or guardian's views should be included within the individual intimate care plan. It is good practice for adults providing intimate care to young people (from the age of 8) to be of the same gender. In certain circumstances and it would usually be unexpected circumstances this good practice principle may need to be waived where failure to provide appropriate care would result in an omission of care.

This is best practice, however, it is recognised that within some services the gender of staff is often made up of predominantly female staff and therefore the same gender principle is often difficult to implement in practice. This needs to be explained to the child and family as part of negotiating the agreed intimate care plan and whatever is put in place should be reviewed and monitored regularly.

**4. Make sure practice in intimate care is as consistent as possible.**

The management of all children who require support with their intimate care needs to be carefully planned. A person centred approach to providing intimate and personal care promotes both individual and consistent patterns of care. The provision of intimate and personal care always has to be considered within the context of the individual person who requires assistance to meet their intimate and personal care needs.

Children/young people who require intimate care should have an individual intimate care plan (this could be within an Individual Education or Health Plan) which sets out the child/young person's views and how they would like their care given, together with specific information to enable care givers to carry out their intimate care. These plans also include a full risk assessment to address issues such as moving and handling, personal safety of the child and the carer. Any individual issues including religious and cultural views will be recorded in these plans. Any historical concerns (such as past abuse) should be noted and taken into account.

The intimate care documentation should be agreed by the young person, parents/carers, designated staff and professionals. The intimate care plan should be reviewed annually or as the child/young person's needs change.

Line managers have a responsibility for ensuring their staff have a consistent approach. This does not mean that everyone has to do everything identically, but approaches should not differ markedly between staff.

Elements of consistency for each individual child include:

- Language – Using recognised words or other cues and agreed terminology
- Physical touch – Always washing intimate parts with a wash tool and not bare hands
- Documentation – Following the child's individual intimate care plan

Consistency of approach can be helped by checking with the child, their carers/ staff who know the child well and reading the child's individual health care plans. If something needs changing in a procedure, it is important to let all those who are involved in their care know about the changes.

**5. Never do something unless you know how to do it.**

All staff who provide intimate care should receive training to promote good practice. No one should ever undertake a task unless they know how to do it. Just because staff or volunteers have done something with their own child, it must not be assumed that they can do it with a child or young person they are providing care for.

Certain intimate care procedures must only be carried out by appropriately trained staff. It is the line manager's responsibility to ensure their staff members are appropriately trained and receive regular updates.

## School Statement of Commitment

…………School is committed to ensuring that all staff responsible for the personal and intimate care of children will undertake their duties in a professional manner at all times.

- The Governing Body will act in accordance with Section 175 of the Education Act 2002 and 'Safeguarding Children in Education' (DfES 2004) to safeguard and promote the welfare of all pupils at this school.

- The Governing Body and Headteacher will act in accordance with the supplementary DfES guidance: 'Safer Recruitment and Selection in Education Settings' (2005) and 'Dealing with Allegations of Abuse against Teachers and other Staff' (2005).

- This school takes seriously its responsibility to safeguard and promote the welfare of the children and young people in its care. Meeting a pupil's intimate care needs is one aspect of safeguarding.

- The Governing Body recognises its duties and responsibilities in relation to the Disability Discrimination Act, which requires that any child with an impairment that affects his/her ability to carry out day-to-day activities must not be discriminated against.

## Sussex Community NHS

NHS Trust

- This Intimate Care Policy should be read in conjunction with the following (Name of school) policies:

  - Child Protection/Safeguarding Policy

  - Health and Safety Policy and procedures

  - Policy for the administration of medicines

  - DCC moving and handling policy

  - Special Educational Needs policy

  - Policy on restrictive physical interventions/appropriate use of force and restraint

  - Staff code of conduct or guidance on safe working practice.

**This school endorses the good practice guidance in intimate care [BHCFS/SCT] and the quality statements will be followed by all school staff.**

**The Quality Statements:**

1. **Treat every child with dignity and respect and ensure privacy**

2. **Involve the child/young person in their own intimate care and be aware of and responsive to the child's reactions**

3. **Encourage the child/young person to have a positive image of their own body**

4. **Make sure practice in intimate care is as consistent as possible**

5. **Never do something unless you know how to do it**

The Good practice guidance will be available to all children, families and staff.

Signed _____Head teacher (etc)

Date_____

## Sussex Community NHS

NHS Trust

**Individual Care Plan: Intimate Care**

Name of child _____

Date of birth _____ Date plan was written _____

Was this care plan discussed with child? YES / NO

if no, please indicate reason

Agreed with parent,

date _____ Signature _____

---

Please describe here the type of intimate care that requires assistance.
*E.g. child soils and requires assistance/supervision with cleaning themselves, disposing of soiled pad / underwear and re-clothing*

---

Does this intimate care procedure require additional training for staff members? YES / NO

If YES, please indicate here who will provide the training and how often staff will need to have refresher training. I.e. Specialist nursing team annually.

Sussex Community **NHS**

NHS Trust

Who will provide the care? Please list staff members trained to provide this care.

Name                                Position/job                        Date of training

Communication/choice.

How is the child going to indicate who they want to assist in their care, when they need assistance and if they have any dislikes relating to their intimate care. This may need to involve the wider multi-disciplinary team (MDT) and the development of their communication system.

Where will this care be provided? Please be specific about identified area.

**Sussex Community NHS**

NHS Trust

Detail here what equipment the child young person may need (i.e. continence pad- size? Catheters, toilet seating etc) and who is responsible for providing it.

What is the child able to do for themselves? This will need to be considered in termly targets as is an area for encouraging learning and promoting independence, no matter how small the participation. Please date each entry.

Any other comments

Agreed by nursery/school etc please sign, print name and designation

Signed _____print _____

Designation_____date_____

## References used in this chapter

Department of Health and Department for Education and Skills (2002) *Guidance on Restrictive Physical Interventions For People With Learning Disability and Autistic Spectrum Disorder, In Health, Education and Social Care Settings.*

BILD (2010) *Code Of Practice for the Use and Reduction of Restrictive Physical Interventions.* Third edition.

Department of Health (2010) *National Framework for Children and Young People's Continuing Care.* http://www.dh.gov.uk/prod_consum_dh/groups/dh_digitalassets/@dh/@en/@ps/documents/digitalasset/dh_116469.pdf

# 5. Working in partnership with parents and carers

Viv Cooper and Gemma Honeyman, Challenging Behaviour Foundation

## Introduction and general principles

Most disabled children live with their families who provide the majority of their care and support. Service providers must therefore engage with the child's family and work in partnership with them to identify shared outcomes and ways of achieving these.

It is important to remember:

- Everyone is working to achieve good outcomes for the individual child.

- There is a greater chance of success if everyone works together in a consistent way.

- Families are powerful advocates for their children, and supporting them in this role through good information and shared goals benefits everyone.

- Families are diverse – there is no such thing as a 'typical' family and their individual circumstances can vary enormously. Understanding the individual family context is essential.

- Families may have had varying experiences of support, advice and information from various different professionals. This could range from extremely positive, supportive experiences, to poor and difficult experiences.

- Information should be accessible and jargon free. Navigating health, education and social care processes can be confusing and it is important to ensure that families have access to good, clear information about your service and that they are encouraged to ask questions at any stage.

Services should be committed to inclusion and will need to take a proactive role to ensure that they develop a good relationship with families. This will include asking parents about their child's support needs and promoting an atmosphere that is open so that parents feel comfortable to share information, safe in the knowledge that:

- it will be communicated to staff who need to know that information

- it will be used sensitively to ensure their child's needs are met

-  it will not be used to exclude their child from the service or from specific activities.

This will require investment of time and effort – both initially and throughout the ongoing partnership, but this investment will greatly enhance a holistic approach to meeting the needs of the child and ensuring that they have a positive experience.

If the service is a mainstream or universal service, systems should be in place to ensure that additional needs including behaviour support are identified as part of the admissions process.

All information about a child will need to be regularly updated as the child's needs change and develop. The review process in education and social services can be a useful time to ensure that information about the child is up to date. However, reviews can be arranged at any time and all partners including parents should be able to trigger a review.

## Diversity

Any family can have a disabled child. The family circumstances can vary greatly, including, for example, the make-up of the family unit, the number and ages of children within it, the age of the parents, their cultural background, their socio-economic status, level of education, living arrangements and employment, and whether they are in good or poor health. All of these factors are important to take into account when supporting the family to work in partnership with staff and carers in order to meet the needs of the child.

Acknowledging and understanding the diversity of families, and the impact these factors have will ensure a greater chance of success when developing a good relationship with the family.

## Working together

Working in partnership should include the following key components:

- developing a good relationship

- agreeing how you will work together, both initially and on an ongoing basis

- agreeing appropriate communication channels

- sharing information about the child

- reviewing and updating information.

As indicated earlier many parents of children with challenging behaviour will have been unfairly criticised for their child's behaviour and may need to be reassured by service providers that they understand that behaviour that challenges, which arises from learning difficulties and or autism, is not caused by poor parenting.

# Developing a good relationship and partnership working

Families consistently report that they want good information, the right support for their disabled child and to be respected as valued partners. It is essential, therefore, that early contact is a positive and supportive experience, which shows that the service values parents as partners who hold key information about supporting their child. Be clear that you want to jointly agree how best to work together. This initial contact will need to set the tone for the relationship and be 'child centred', and tailored to individual need – for example, a home visit, or an appointment to visit the service at a time that suits the family. The key message to parents is that the service will work in partnership with them, and jointly agree how to work together with a good two-way communication process to ensure a holistic approach.

Once the important first contact has been established, the outcome should be a clear understanding from the parents and the service about working together to agreed aims, sharing information and good communication strategies. Working in partnership is a relationship that needs to develop – if it is built on a firm foundation it is more likely to succeed and be sustained.

A useful approach is 'co-production' where all stakeholders, including family members and professionals, are considered as partners with a valued contribution to make. They jointly agree what is required then work together to put in place what is needed. More detail on this approach is given in Chapter 10 on training.

# Sharing information

In order to successfully work in partnership, parents and services will need to share information about the child. How information is exchanged will depend on the individual child and family (for example, adjustments will need to be made if English is not the first language). Whichever format is used, the following essential headings should be covered (some areas will overlap):

- The child: including likes, dislikes, interests and support needs.

- Important people (family and friends) in the child's life (and the roles they play).

- Important people (professionals) who provide support.

- Communication – how does the child communicate? What augmentative communication is used? Are communication aids used?

- Health information: including any diagnosis, health support needs, equipment, mobility, food and nutrition. Contact details of professionals supporting the child and family, and what level of support they provide.

- Personal care and support needs.

- Environmental issues: sensory considerations, health and safety, specialist adaptations and equipment, adaptations to home environment.

- Positive behaviour support: (is there a behaviour support plan in place?) types of behaviour displayed, including level of frequency and duration.

- Other family considerations.

The information gathered can be used to create a 'personal communication passport' (details at the end of the chapter) or an 'All About Me' book. These provide a practical and child-centred approach to passing on key information in a clear, positive and accessible format. The terms personal communication passport and 'All About Me' book are often used interchangeably. In practice passports are often more adult focused, used to pass on key information about a child and tend to be slightly more concise.

Communication dictionaries focus solely on communication styles and provide a means of interpreting non-verbal communication in children with severe communication impairments. The information contained in a dictionary would usually also be included in an 'All About Me' book or a personal communication passport. Often 'All About Me' books and personal communication passports are simply used to share information, but they can also be used as a central tool in person-centred planning.

An example of a school passport from Torfield School is shown at the end of the chapter on communication (Chapter 9) alongside an example of an 'All About Me' form from White Lodge Centre, in Chertsey, Surrey.

Families will have a wealth of information about their child and it is important to devise a method whereby the essential information is recorded and made available to every staff member who will support the child. A one page summary with key points can be a useful tool for the wider staff team, with more detailed information to supplement this made available to staff who regularly work with the child. Increasingly, use is being made of smart phone and web based apps to support communication. Early Support have developed an app that is a smart phone and web-based interactive version of the Early Support Family Held Record (www.councilfordisabledchildren.org.uk/earlysupport).

A useful way to get a holistic account of the child's support needs is to ask the parents to describe in detail a typical day, from when their child wakes, to when he/she goes to bed at night. This will enable a complete picture of their support needs and a greater understanding of the perspective of the family and the needs of other family members (for example, it may be really important that on a particular day a sibling attends an after school club, so activities with the family at that time will need to fit round this).

# Regular communication with parents/carer

A home/school communication book can be incredibly helpful to support both the relationship with parents and understanding of the child. Regular input from parents can flag up whether the child is particularly tired, has slept well or may have some health issues, all of which can impact on behaviour. It can be particularly useful to include photographs or examples of activities, from home to school or vice versa, as a way of sharing information, which children can participate in, and promoting communication. Use of texts and emails can be another way to support this contact and share information further.

> **Communicating with parents: top tips**
> Ask parents about their aspirations for their child
>
> - remember that parents are the experts on their child
> - be clear, accurate and open
> - be an active and empathic listener
> - be approachable and accessible
> - find out which methods of communication are preferred by parents
> - seek out the child's views
> - keep communication channels open – even if you disagree
> - signpost parents to further information and sources of independent advice.
>
> (Adapted from *Working Effectively with Parents: A training guide for SEN caseworkers* (2010) Department for Children, Schools and Families)

# Consent to behaviour plans

Parents must be fully involved in the process of drawing up the positive behaviour support plan (as detailed in Chapter 8), in conjunction with other professionals who are involved with the child and who can meaningfully contribute to the support plan. Parents will also be the major provider of information in building up a communication picture (Chapter 9).

Where services and parents are using different strategies every effort should be made to agree on a consistent approach for the benefit of the child/young person. Service providers should be aware that parents are rarely provided with quality information and training on challenging behaviour and service providers should consider providing information and involving families in training alongside their staff. This helps to ensure that everyone is working from the same starting point and reduces the likelihood of disputes arising. It also reduces the likelihood of behaviour issues being ineffectively addressed because of a failure to adopt a common approach.

At the end of the process of engaging parents in designing a positive behaviour support plan, parents should be asked to sign the plan to consent to the strategies detailed in the plan being used with their child. A copy of this should be kept by the service on the child's file and parents should also be given a copy.

Part of the monitoring and review process (outlined in Chapter 13) will include reviewing whether or not the behaviour support plan is still relevant and whether or not it needs amending. Each time changes or additions are made, parents should be asked to sign to consent to the updated plan.

*Mary has a 12-year-old son, Jonathan, who has severe learning disabilities and behaviour described as challenging.*

*In the past Mary had just been given copies of behaviour support plans by his school and asked to sign them to give her consent. She was asked to consent to Jonathan being restrained in the prone position (face down). Mary was not happy with this as she doesn't restrain Jonathan at home and felt that other strategies could be used. The school said they would exclude Jonathan if Mary didn't sign the plan. Mary reluctantly signed the consent form as she was worried that Jonathan might have to go to a residential school if he was excluded. Jonathan was restrained approximately 10 times a month.*

*After a change of headteacher, Mary was asked to attend a meeting to review the behaviour support plan. Mary and the teaching staff reviewed incident forms and discussed what worked and what didn't. Mary and the staff learnt a lot from talking to each other and sharing what was already working. Mary took some of the laminated symbols used to communicate with Jonathan at school to use at home. Staff agreed that they would look for the 'early warning signs' that Mary described such as flicking his fingers quickly and reduced eye contact.*

*The headteacher listened to her concerns about restraint and explained that he had a duty to keep the other children in the school safe. As a result the plan was changed so that as a last resort a two-person escort would be used instead, which Mary agreed was less restrictive. Mary was happy to sign two copies of the behaviour support plan to show her consent and was given a copy to keep.*

*Three months later they met again to review the plan. The frequency of Jonathan's challenging behaviour had decreased and he had only been restrained twice in this period. It wasn't all good news as a new behaviour had emerged so they focused on developing specific strategies for this.*

## Other forms of consent

Some children and young people may be on regular medication for a health condition such as asthma or epilepsy. Where this is the case and routine medication will need to be given while the child is in receipt of a service, parents must give their full written consent.

For some children the need for additional therapy such as physio or speech and language may have been identified. Again, where this is the case, parents must give their full written consent for either referral to or receipt of such therapies.

## Maintaining the partnership

The partnership is an ongoing relationship. Regular dialogue and information sharing is essential to ensure all are up to date and working together. Regular communication will also ensure that any difficulties are identified and addressed early before they become major issues. Remember it is very important to share what is working well too!

Parents, service providers, staff and carers should work together in the spirit of co-production to jointly agree:

- the format and content of the child's care plan – this will include details about the child's communication (Chapter 9) and a positive behaviour support plan (Chapter 8)

- how and when the plan will be regularly reviewed

- regular communication methods between home and the service

- how other key information and updates will be shared.

## Conclusion

Working in partnership with families to deliver good outcomes for the child is a priority. Parents provide the main source of love and care for the child and are a valuable source of information and expertise. Investment in developing and maintaining a good relationship with the child's family will be mutually beneficial and greatly enhance a holistic, consistent and outcomes focused approach to supporting the child.

### References used in this chapter

Department for Children, Schools and Families (2010) *Working Effectively with Parents: A Training Guide for SEN Caseworkers.*

Communication Passports – person centred approach to gather and present information about children and young people. Free templates are available at http://www.communicationpassports.org.uk

# 6. Promoting a partnership with the child

As well as working in partnership with parents, services should work in partnership with children and young people who have behaviour that challenges. All children and young people have the right to participate in decisions that affect them, and this includes children and young people with learning disabilities, behaviour that challenges and communication needs. Working with children and young people from the start using person-centred planning ensures that they are at the centre of the process, and focuses on their strengths and abilities and what support they need to achieve, using, for example, the Planning for the Future Information Sheet (Challenging Behaviour Foundation). This is vital to effectively follow and manage any strategies laid out in their behaviour management plan.

Understanding how the child or young person communicates is key to such partnership working. It is important to remember that 'challenging behaviour' is the way in which a child or young person with severe learning disability or on the autistic spectrum communicates. This may include communicating things they want – an activity, a particular item, attention and so on – or things they wish to avoid or escape, such as an uncomfortable sensation, a demand to do something, unwanted affection, and so on. This is why gathering information on the child at an early stage is so important, so that staff can learn to recognise triggers and early warning signs in order to try to find out what the child is trying to say and, in so doing, prevent challenging behaviour escalating.

## Consultation

A number of government policies and guidance place legislative duties and obligations on services to consult with children and give them a greater say in the way their care and support is delivered (Franklin 2013). For example:

- The United Nations Convention on the Rights of the Child (UNCRC) adopted and ratified by the UK government in 1991 is often seen as creating the driver towards the increased participation of children and young people.

- Guidance and regulations within the Children Act 1989 make it clear that, if a child has complex needs, communication needs or severe learning disabilities, arrangements must be made to establish their views, and that a disabled child cannot be assumed to be incapable of sharing in decision-making.

- The Children Act (2004) reinforces children's right to be listened to by service providers.

- The UN Convention on the Rights of Persons with Disabilities (UNCRPD) (2006) embodies the participation of disabled people, including children.

- Statutory guidance on the role of Lead Members requires them to regularly consult children and young people and stresses the need for participation at a local level (DCSF 2009).

In addition the The Children and Families Act 2014 introduces section 19, which states that when delivering services local authorities must have regard to the views, wishes and feelings of the child or young person; the importance of the child or young person participating as fully as possible; and the importance of the child or young person being provided with the information and support necessary to enable participation in those decisions.

The UN Convention on the Rights of Persons with Disabilities, article 7, states that disabled children and young people's participation should happen at individual, service and strategic levels; and should take into account the child or young person's age and maturity, on an equal basis with other children, and they should be provided with disability and age-appropriate assistance to realise that right.

- At an **individual level** children and young people make personal decisions relating to their own care and support. For example, this could include formal mechanisms such as review process, or informal choices and decisions such as what activities they want to be involved in, when they want to be quiet and be on their own, what strategies and rewards will be used to support their behaviour, and what sanctions might be used to manage their behaviour.

> In order to support the development of meaningful partnerships between parents, short break carers and young people, staff at Barnardo's Family Link Plus in Brighton and Hove have been developing a feedback form as part of the annual Review of Short Break Carers. Based on discussions with a young person, her parent and short break carer, the supervising social worker was able to individualise the form to reflect her specific interests and to address her communication needs. Feedback from the young person and the parent on this piece of work has been very positive. The parent stated that '...[the young person] was delighted and excited to receive her own mail that she could open, read and complete herself'.

- At a **service level** children and young people should have opportunities to give their views about the services they use, or the strategic planning of services. This can take place as one-off time limited consultation events, for example a focus group, or as ongoing consultation through the involvement in strategic planning and consultation forums.

The VIPER Research project was a three year Big Lottery funded project that trained disabled young people to work as researchers and to look at the participation of disabled children and young people in decision-making about services. They found a number of examples of the impact that participation had had on services. One leisure centre reported that it had improved its publicity about accessible activities, set up new activities and purchased accessible equipment. Another project had also influenced changes to local leisure services, bringing about an increase in the number of sports and leisure activities available for disabled young people and improvements to local facilities, such as accessible changing rooms. Other practical changes mentioned were the introduction of 'Stay Safe Cards' (giving information on safe locations to go to if young people are worried when out in their community) and improvements to sex education.

Helping disabled children make decisions may often mean that services need to find creative and informal ways of obtaining their views and preferences, for example using observation, art, drama, photography, play or storytelling (see Participation Works: *How to use creative methods for Participation*, 2007).

It should be noted that informal methods such as these should not be seen as less valuable than formal participation methods. Informal opportunities to make everyday choices are key to supporting disabled children and young people to take more control over the support they receive; and later to effectively participate in formal decisions and processes that affect them.

# Process of decision making

Participating in decisions is a process rather than a single action taking place at one moment in time. The first three elements of this process are used in the Mental Capacity Act 2005 when assessing a person's capacity to make decisions. The usual decision making process is made up of the following elements:

- **Information** - Being given information to understand what has happened or information on which to base a decision (informed choice).

- **Cognitive process** - Weighing up different options and making a choice.

- **Expression** - Expressing one's decision or views.

- **Action feedback** - Receiving acknowledgement or feedback on one's views or decisions or having one's decisions acted upon.

This means that making decisions is affected by three processes:

- **Comprehension** - Ability to understand and retain information.

- **Cognitive ability** - Ability to weigh up information and reach a decision.

- **Communication** - Ability to communicate the decision made (Carlin 2009).

All children and young people can and do communicate and those children and young people with communication impairments have the same rights as other children and young people to participate in decision making. Recognising and understanding children and young people's access to language and communication methods is the first step in supporting their participation (Participation Works 2007).

Disabled children who do not use formal language to communicate may use an alternative form of communication (for example, PECS, symbols or signs) or will communicate in an individual way through behaviour, or through gestures and noises.

Using language differently or in ways that are individual to them may mean that many disabled children and young people with significant support or communication needs may require additional support to access the 'usual process' of making decisions due to the way that information is typically presented.

Therefore it is vital that services ensure information provided to young people is available in a range of accessible formats and a range of accessible methods (see chapter 9 on Communication) are used to ensure that all children can participate in decision making, have a say in the way their support is given and what strategies will be used to manage their behaviour.

It is incredibly important not to underestimate a child or young person's capacity to participate based on their communication skills. The Council for Disabled Children recently carried out research with children and young people to find out which health outcomes they prioritised. We included five young people in the research who participated using talking mats and were clearly able to identify and indicate their health priorities (Morris and others 2014).

There are a wide range of resources available to support consultation and participation with children and young people who are disabled or who have special educational needs and disabilities, for example:

- Participation Works (2010) *How to support disabled and non-disabled children and young people to work together in inclusive groups**

- Participation Works (2009) How to involved children and young people with communication impairments in decision making*

- Council for Disabled Children (2009) *Making Ourselves Heard: Exploring disabled children's participation* (available to buy at http://shop.ncb.org.uk)

- Participation Works and Council for Disabled Children (2008) *Top Tips for Participation: What disabled young people want**

- Triangle (2001) *Two Way Street* (available to buy at http://www.triangle.org.uk/catalog/resources/cds-dvds-and-videos/two-way-street-handbook-and-dvd)

- Kids (2009) *Our Play - Our Choice: A Kids consultation with disabled children* (www.kids.org.uk)

- The Children's Society & Triangle (2008) *I Can Tell You What I Want*

- The Children's Society (2008) *Ask Us - We're Included* (Part of Disability Toolkit)

- The Children's Society (2008) *My Life, My Decisions, My Choice* (Part of Disability Toolkit)

- *The Children's Society Disability Toolkit: An online, interactive resource for practitioners to share information and resources for working with disabled children and young people.* (http://sites.childrenssociety.org.uk/disabilitytoolkit/toolkit/)

- Triangle (2012) *Getting It Right* ( available to buy at http://www.triangle.org.uk/catalog/resources/consultation-reports-and-handbooks/getting-it-right-2012)

* Available on the Participation Works website (www.participationworks.org.uk/) where there are also resources providing specific guidance for children with speech, language and communication needs.

There are also resources providing specific guidance for children with communication needs (see www.participationworks.org.uk).

## Children and young people giving consent

Wherever possible or appropriate to their understanding, children and young people should be involved in developing their behaviour support plan in a person-centred way so that they understand the sanctions and techniques that the service will use to manage their behaviour. Where this is not possible, it is essential that the service has a clear understanding of how the child or young person communicates and what the child or young person is communicating by their behaviour. There is more detail on this in Chapter 9, which focuses on communication.

This is a complex area. Following is a flow diagram that captures the key elements and their implications for capacity to consent. However, this area is underpinned by a number of pieces of legislation, legal precedence and guidance.

These include:
- *The legal aspects of the care and treatment of children and young people with mental disorder*
- *Reference guide to consent for examination or treatment*
- the Mental Capacity Act 2005
- the Family Law Reform Act 1969.

Particular regard must be given to young people aged 17 and over in order to comply with the Mental Capacity Act 2005 which, although it generally applies to adults (those over the age of 18 years), does give young people aged 16–17 the right to consent. However, where young people in this age group refuse to give consent, this may in certain circumstances be overridden by their parents or the court. In other words, they have the right to say 'yes' but not the right to say 'no' – as consent can be sought from another source. In relation to children and young people under the age of 16 years the Act states that they have the right to take part in consent decisions – in line with their age and level of understanding.

In order to determine whether or not disabled young people can exercise their right to consent, their capacity is assessed. When assessing capacity to make a decision or give consent it must be remembered that it is a 'time and decision specific test' – in other words the young person may be able to make some decisions and not others, or may be able to make a decision one day but not the following day. Assessing their capacity is based on whether or not they can understand and retain the information relevant to the decision, their ability to use or weigh up that information and their ability to communicate their decision.

If a disabled child or young person does not have capacity to make a decision or give consent, then that is generally done by their parents or whoever has parental responsibility. All decisions or giving of consent must be done with the child's best interests at the centre of the process.

The flow diagram and the italicised paragraphs that follow are extracted from pp.202 – 3 of *Disabled Children: a legal handbook* (Legal Action Group 2010)© by Steve Broach, Luke Clements and Janet Read, available at www.lag.org.uk.

Is it contemplated that treatment may be given in a psychiatric unit in relation to a mental disorder under the Mental Health Act (MHA) 1983?

**Yes** → The treatment can be given (even without consent) under the MHA 1983 but consent should still be sought.

**No** ↓

Is the child aged 16 or 17?*

**Yes** → The child is assumed to be capable of giving consent, but a refusal can be overridden*. If the child is shown to lack capacity to make the particular decision then a 'best interests' decision will need to be made on his or her behalf. This means that whoever is making a decision or taking any action on that person's behalf must do this in the person's best interests.

**No** ↓

Is the child 'Gillick competent'?
A Gillick competent child is a child who has attained sufficient understanding and intelligence to be able to understand fully what is involved in the proposed intervention.

**Yes** → The child is regarded as competent to consent to a particular intervention but if they refuse treatment then this decision can be overridden as above.

**No** ↓

Is the decision within the zone of parental control?
The zone of parental control is not a straightforward concept and clinicians are advised to be cautious about relying on the consent of a parent if there is any indication that he or she is not acting in the best interests of the child.

**Yes** → A person with parental responsibility for the child may make the decision on the child's behalf – although this can be challenged by way of an application to the court for a declaration as to his or her 'best interests'.

**No** ↓

If the decision is urgent then the responsible clinician can give emergency treatment but otherwise consideration should be given to making an application to the court for a declaration as to his or her 'best interests'.

*The law on consent to treatment, including treatment for mental disorder, for young people (aged 16 – 17 years) is governed by the Mental Capacity Act (MCA) 2005 and Family Law Reform Act (FLRA) 1969 s8. The MCA 2005 creates a rebuttable presumption that all individuals aged 16 or over have capacity to make decisions for themselves.*

*For 16- to 17-year-olds, the MCA 2005 presumption of capacity to make decisions has to be considered in the context of FLRA 1969 s8. This provides that persons of this age can consent to any surgical, medical or dental treatment. The courts have, however, distinguished between the right to consent and the right to refuse – and held that in certain cases a court (or even a parent) can override a refusal by such a child (e.g. Re: R (A minor) (Wardship: Medical Treatment) (1992)). While it is questionable whether the case law based on FLRA 1969 s8 is still good law (preceding as it did the enactment of MCA 2005), it is nevertheless the case that the courts, in the exercise of their wardship powers, can override certain treatment refusal decisions of 16- and 17-year-olds even if the young person is 'Gillick competent'.*

*The same process should be used by services – other than health – when making decisions about the child's capacity to consent to medication and other clinical procedures or whether the parents should give that consent.*

## Carers Trust – National Personal Care Procedures states:

### CONSENT

#### 1.0 CONSENT FOR CARE
1.1 If a child or young person is competent to give consent for care themselves then it will be sought directly from them. The legal position regarding "competence" is different for children aged under 16 and young people aged 16 and 17.

#### 1.1 Children aged under 16
1.1.1 There is no specific legal age when a child becomes competent to consent to treatment or care; it depends both on the child and the seriousness or complexity of the treatment or care being proposed. Children aged under 16 are deemed competent to give valid consent to care if they have "sufficient understanding and intelligence to enable him or her to understand fully what is proposed" (sometimes known as "Gillick competence").

1.1.2 If a child under 16 is competent to consent for himself or herself it is still good practice to involve their parent / person with parental responsibility in decision-making, unless the child specifically asks you not to and cannot be persuaded otherwise.

1.1.3 If a child under 16 is not competent to make a particular decision, then their parent / person with parental responsibility can take that decision for them, although the child should still be involved as much as possible.

continued

## 1.2 Young people aged 16 and 17

1.2.1 Once children reach the age of 16 they are presumed in law to be competent to give consent for themselves. This means that in many respects they need to be treated like adults – for example if a signature is required on a consent form they can sign for themselves if able to do so. However, it is still good practice to involve their parent / person with parental responsibility in decision-making unless the child or young person asks you not to.

1.2.2 If young people of 16 or 17 are not competent to take a particular decision, then their parent / person with parental responsibility can make that decision for them, although the young person needs to be involved as much as possible.

1.2.3 When deciding if a young person aged 16 or 17 lacks capacity to make a specific decision, the principles contained within the Mental Capacity Act 2005 can be applied. Please refer to the adult's personal care procedure (B01b) section 4.0 for details.

## 1.3 'Best interests'

1.3.1 Any decisions taken on behalf of a child or young person who is not competent to take the decision themselves or who lacks the mental capacity to do so, must be taken in the child or young person's best interests, in consultation with their parent / person with parental responsibility.

1.3.2 In some cases multi-disciplinary 'best interest' meeting may be held, comprising professionals involved in the care of the child or young person, their parent / carer / close family members as appropriate. A decision will be made as to the benefits of the proposed care and a resolution made as to how that care will be provided if it is decided that it is in the child or young person's best interests to provide it. The outcome of the 'best interests' meeting will be recorded in the child or young person's file and all necessary information regarding the provision of personal care entered into their care plan.

## 1.4 Written consent

1.4.1 Crossroads Care requires written consent for all care provided. A model care plan that can be used by schemes and which incorporates an appropriate consent form is available at CT.03.

1.4.2 Written consent can be given by a competent child or young person and / or the child or young person's parent / person with parental responsibility as appropriate.

# Consent – information sharing

Personal information about children and families held by professionals is subject to a duty of confidence, and should normally not be disclosed without consent. However, the information may be passed to someone else with the individual's consent for a particular purpose, for instance to other professionals involved in their care or treatment or for research purposes.

Where information is shared, there is an implied understanding that the information will not be used except where it is strictly needed to help the professional provide the service. Each member of the team, and any person who provides administrative or secretarial support, has an obligation to treat the information as confidential.

Confidentiality and consent should, where possible, be introduced and discussed with children and young people to ensure they understand their rights (including refusal, withdrawal or partial withdrawal of consent) and staff responsibilities. Personal information on children and young people is ordinarily subject to a legal duty of confidence, and should not normally be disclosed without the person's consent. However, where there are concerns that a child is or may be at risk of significant harm, disclosure of information may be necessary to safeguard the well-being of the child.

Children and young people should, where possible, be made aware of these conditions before giving their consent and all services and organisations should have clear policies in place for staff on how to deal with safeguarding issues.

## References used in this chapter

Broach, S, Clements, L and Read, J (2010) *Disabled Children: A legal handbook.* London: Legal Action Group.

Carlin, J (2009) Managing My Way: background paper. Associate Consultant Council for Disabled Children.

Challenging Behaviour Foundation 'Planning for the Future Information Sheet'. http://www.challengingbehaviour.org.uk/learning-disability-files/15_Planning-for-the-future.pdf

DCSF (2009) *The Roles and Responsibilities of the Lead Member for Children's Services and the Director of Children's Services*

DfES/DH Information for parents (2006) *Autistic spectrum disorders and related conditions.* https://www.education.gov.uk/publications/standard/publicationdetail/page1/ES12

Franklin A (2013) *VIPER, A literature review on the participation of disabled children and young people in decision making.* London: Alliance for Inclusive Education, Council for Disabled Children, National Children's Bureau and the Children's Society.

Morris, C, Janssens, A, Allard, A and Shilling, V (2013) *Informing the NHS Outcomes Framework: what outcomes of NHS care should be measured for children with neurodisability?* National Institute for Health Research.

NICE (2011) Clinical Guideline: *Autism: recognition, referral and diagnosis of children and young people on the autism spectrum.* http://www.nice.org.uk/nicemedia/live/13572/56424/56424.pdf

Participation Works (2007) *How to use creative methods for Participation.* http://www.participationworks.org.uk/resources/how-to-use-creative-methods-for-participation

Shaw, C, Brady, LM and Davey, C (2011) *Guidelines for Research with Children and Young People.* London: National Children's Bureau.

# 7. Plans

For children with higher levels of need, the overarching plan is a statement or education, health and care plan. From September 2014 statements of SEN will be replaced by education, health and care plans (EHC plans). The majority of the provisions in relation to EHC plans remain broadly the same as for statements. The threshold for an EHC plan is the same as for a statement – effectively that a school is unable to meet a child or young person's special educational needs. However, a plan may continue up to the age of 25 if the young person is in education, training or an apprenticeship. Plans will also continue for 16 – 17 year olds if they are not in education, employment or training. The EHC plan sets out a child or young person's special educational needs, their aspirations, views and interests, the outcomes sought for them and the special educational provision, healthcare provision and social care provision required.

Alongside a child's statement or EHC plan may sit a number of specialist plans. Local practice will differ from one area of the country to the next. In some places children will have separate plans to cover each area of specialist support – for example a healthcare plan, an emergency plan, a moving and handling plan etc. In other regions, a child will have a single plan and where additional support is required this information will form a part or module of that single plan. The arrangement will usually have developed in a specific way due to historical and practical factors in each area of the country.

The important issue is that if disabled children require additional assistance in specific areas of care or support, the information explaining how the support should be given needs to be written down and shared with all those who are offering this support. Each child should have an individual plan that is specific to their particular needs. Plans will vary in length and complexity, depending on the needs of an individual child. All plans will be read and used by family carers and a range of staff so they should be written using jargon-free, non-medical language that is easy to understand. The partnership arrangement developed in a geographic area should detail the format of plans to be used.

If disabled children are fostered or use overnight short breaks, the use of plans to cover their care and support is outlined in statutory guidance (the *Children Act 1989 Guidance and Regulations. Volume 2: Care Planning, Placement and Case review; and Short Breaks Statutory guidance on how to safeguard and promote the welfare of disabled children using short breaks*; DCSF 2010). Disabled children receiving overnight short breaks under Section 17 (Children Act 1989) require a 'child in need plan' and for those having overnight short breaks under Section 20, where regulation 48 applies, a 'short break plan' is written. There is no set template for either of these plans, but the information to be covered is stipulated in the guidance. This means that where disabled children who have behaviour that is described as challenging are using short breaks, the information covering the specialist support required may be in the form of a single plan or the child may have a 'short break plan' plus a number of specialist plans. Details of templates that can be used are on the Council for Disabled Children website:

http://www.councilfordisabledchildren.org.uk/resources/cdcs-resources/short-breaks-training-materials/model-short-breaks-care-plans

The group of disabled children covered by this publication may require healthcare plans – covering their clinical procedures and medication. Some children with complex needs also have moving and handling plans, as well as emergency plans. It is also important that their level and mode of communication is included in any detailed care plans. As outlined above, these plans may be separate documents or may form a part or module of a single plan.

The final element of the Checklist for inclusion is the building in of a process of regular monitoring and review. It is important to remember that the support needs of children who have behaviour that is described as challenging do constantly change as they grow and develop, benefit from positive support strategies and meet new challenges. Ensuring good knowledge of their interests, needs and abilities as well as their communication preferences can work well to prevent or de-escalate challenging behaviours.

This chapter provides information on what services need to continually monitor and review in order to successfully continue to provide a service to this group of children.

## Written records

It is essential that services maintain ongoing records not only to comply with regulations and standards but to ensure that they are continuing to provide a safe service for both children and staff. The following is a checklist of the kinds of written records that services need to hold when including children who have behaviour that is described as challenging.

- When medication has been administered. An example of the form used by the short break service in Gloucestershire is at the end of this chapter.

- When a physical intervention has been used to prevent a child or young person harming themselves or others.

- When an incident occurred where a child or young person potentially or actually injured themselves or others.

- Details of when staff or carers have received initial training and who has provided it.

- Details of when the training has been updated and when it is next due.

- If a child uses any equipment, logs should be kept detailing when it was serviced and maintained. This includes ensuring that equipment in a child's own home is maintained regularly if that is where service provision takes place.

- If a child or young person's needs cannot be met because of their behavioural challenges or moving and handling requirements or if they cannot join in with activities because of their support needs, this should be recorded and discussed at the child's review. These records should contribute in a positive way to future service planning and to ensuring that the service becomes more inclusive over time.

It is important to apply a principle of proportionality to the records that front-line staff are required to keep so that they are not spending an unreasonable amount of time on record keeping and away from direct contact with children and young people.

Where service provision takes place away from the service base, for example in a child's own home or the home of a short break carer, robust systems need to be in place to ensure that the written records of staff and carers are regularly added to the child's main file.

## Written information

The amount and detail of information gathered and stored by a service should be proportionate to the level of service that the child or young person is receiving. It is essential that information is gathered from the child's parents, other significant family members and other settings that the child attends to ensure consistency. Information should include:

- An 'All About Me' book or 'personal communication passport' to include the child or young person's likes or dislikes (examples are given in Chapter 9). These provide a practical and child-centred approach to passing on key information in a clear, positive and accessible format.

- Contact details of family members, other key professionals involved and who to contact in an emergency.

- Information on the child's preferred method of communication – this information may form part of their personal communication passport. It is also useful for services to have information on where staff can go to obtain additional support or resources if the child uses an alternative form of communication, such as Makaton or a symbol system.

- A care plan – this could be a single plan with specialist plans attached as modules of that single plan. Specialist plans may include positive behaviour plans, moving and handling plans, emergency healthcare plans etc. (Information on positive behaviour support plans and examples can be found in Chapter 8.)

- Specialist plans (as listed above) – these can either be part of the main care plan or separate plans. Services may need help to write some of these. For example, assistance from a learning disability nurse and parents to write a positive behaviour plan detailing the strategies for supporting a child or young person; or help from a physiotherapist to write a moving and handling plan. Smaller services will usually want to use and adapt the plans written by larger services.

- Risk assessments that may be specific to children and young people who have behaviour that is considered challenging. (See Chapter 8 for further information on risk assessments and examples of forms.)

- Information on any regular medication that needs to be administered, verified by a medical practitioner. At the end of the chapter is an example of a letter sent out by a short breaks team in Gloucestershire to obtain information from the GP as well as the medication and diet forms used by that service.

  - If the type of medication or dosage changes, services must be notified in writing. This often causes difficulties for services where children may see a healthcare professional during the week and medication is changed with immediate effect. Some services and some doctors have introduced a 'pro-forma' letter, which can be signed by the doctor during the clinic appointment and given to services immediately. A copy of the letter used in Nottingham is at the end of this chapter.

  - Parental consent to the giving of medication and positive behaviour strategies, including physical intervention. (See Chapter 6 for more information on consent.)

## Review

In order to successfully continue to provide a service to children, services need to regularly review their plans, including:

- Reviewing the child or young person's care plan, in particular the positive behaviour support plan and the moving and handling plan if there is one. It is essential that the child's parents and other settings that the child attends are involved in this review process to ensure consistency. Wherever possible therefore, there should be one review across the services the child or young person attends. The frequency of reviews may be governed by legislation, for example for a child receiving overnight short breaks, but where there is no legal requirement, such as a child attending an after-school club, it is good practice to review the plan every six months, or sooner if required.

- Reviewing the written information held on the child to check for changes and updates, for example contact details, medication etc. This is likely to be part of any review process required by legislation. If there are no legal requirements on reviewing, it is good practice to review written information every six months.

- Reviewing the risk assessment to ensure that all risk has been reduced to the lowest possible level. Good practice is to review the risk assessment every six months or sooner if required.

- Reviewing support staff and carers to ensure that they continue to be competent and confident in the positive support strategies detailed in the child's plan and to carry out a physical intervention.

- Reviewing what training has been provided to individual staff members and carers during the previous year so that refresher training and new training needs can be identified.

## Resource examples

Gloucestershire – Medication Form

### TOP TIPS

Name: xxxxx                                    DOB:

---

**MEDICATION INFORMATION**

If xxxxx is having a seizure she will go very quiet – her eyes will be wide open, her pupils dilated; she starts to shake and goes very stiff. This will last
30-40 seconds – she will then generally go to sleep.
7.5mg Buccal Midazolam should be administered for seizure episodes lasting more than 5 minutes in duration or if there are more than 3 brief seizure episodes within 1 hour, or more than 5 in a 2-hour duration.

---

**Physical Description & Health**
- xxxxx has Rett Syndrome and is on the autistic spectrum
- xxxxx is on medication to control her seizures – Keppra (administered at home) and emergency medication Buccal Midazolam – NB: since using Keppra in December 2010, xxxxx has had no seizure clusters (as of 6 June 20XX)
- xxxxx can lack co-ordination

**Personal, Social & Emotional**
- xxxxx wears pads – when soiled lay her down to change
- NB: xxxxx will smear and is very quick, so adults need to be aware!
- xxxxx can be over-friendly
- When out walking hold her hand – she likes dogs (if dog owner allows OK to stroke the dog)
- Needs close supervision during meal times – she will overeat and take other people's food from their plates

**Communication & Language**
- xxxxx uses MAC switches at school
- xxxxx will eye-point
- Staff at school are using Makaton with her – as yet she has not responded but Dad happy for us to use Makaton
- Uses objects of reference, i.e. nappy for toilet time

**Likes**
- Dancing
- Sand (but will eat)
- Jingle ring
- Books to touch and feel
- Listening and dancing to music and nursery rhymes
- TV
- Slapstick actions and noises
- Interaction with staff
- Farm animal noises
- Water
- Outside play/garden
- Sensory Room
- Glueing

**Dislikes**
- Painting
- Roundabouts

July 20XX

# Recording Chart
# for All Medication Administered

Child's Name .............................................................

Date of Birth .............................................................

Any Known Allergies/Sensitivities..............................

...........................................................................

(Use in conjunction with child/young person's individual care plan)

## Note:

Check!! Right child, Right drug, Right dose, Right time and Right Route - **BEFORE** administering **ANY** medication.

Child/young Person's Name ..................................................................... D.O.B. ............................

| Generic Medication Name, Type, Strength and Dose to be given as prescribed | Date & Time | Sign | Date & Time | Sign | Date & Time | Sign |
|---|---|---|---|---|---|---|
| | | | | | | |
| | | | | | | |
| | | | | | | |
| | | | | | | |
| | | | | | | |
| VIA | Instructions: | | | | | |

| Generic Medication Name, Type, Strength and Dose to be given as prescribed | Date & Time | Sign | Date & Time | Sign | Date & Time | Sign |
|---|---|---|---|---|---|---|
| | | | | | | |
| | | | | | | |
| | | | | | | |
| | | | | | | |
| | | | | | | |
| VIA | Instructions: | | | | | |

| Generic Medication Name, Type, Strength and Dose to be given as prescribed | Date & Time | Sign | Date & Time | Sign | Date & Time | Sign |
|---|---|---|---|---|---|---|
| | | | | | | |
| | | | | | | |
| | | | | | | |
| | | | | | | |
| | | | | | | |
| VIA | Instructions: | | | | | |

MH4

Family Link
Jordans Brook House
North Upton Lane
Barnwood
Gloucester GL4 3TL
Fax: 01452372537

**Please ask for:**     JP                          **Phone:** 01452 618XXX

**Our Ref:**     JP PG/                          **Date:**

**Child's Name:**

**D.O.B:**

**Address:**

Dear GP

I am a Paediatric Nurse working for Family Link which is a service that provides short-term breaks for children with disabilities. In order to improve our practice and verify medical information, please can you send/fax a printout medical history for the above named child. I request where possible that this includes:

- The child's diagnosis and/or medical condition
- A record of illnesses and surgical procedures
- All regularly prescribed medication (please complete form enclosed, stating whether the child/young person can manage their own medication safely)
- Medical devices in use
- Immunisation record and any precautions required for safe care practice in the community

A copy of the Medical Authority Form which includes parents' consent to share information is enclosed for your reference.

A pre-paid envelope has been provided for the return of forms enclosed.

Yours sincerely
Miss J Pxxxxxx

Family Link Nurse
Children's Centre
City Hospital Campus
Hucknall Road
Nottingham
NG5 1PB
Tel: 0115 88XXXXX

# URGENT INFORMATION REGARDING MEDICATION

Re: (Child's details)

This patient was reviewed in clinic today and the following medication was started or changed:

Yours sincerely

Signature:

Print Name:

Date:

# 8. Positive behaviour support plans

Viv Cooper and Gemma Honeyman, Challenging Behaviour Foundation

## Positive behaviour support

Children whose behaviour is described as challenging are at greater risk of exclusion and being subjected to restrictive practices such as restraint and seclusion. It is therefore essential that positive behaviour support is addressed at an early stage in order to support the child to achieve their potential and have a good quality of life.

Historically, aversive strategies were used to decrease challenging behaviour such as squirting lemon juice in a child's mouth or spraying them in the face with a water mist. In addition, there was often a narrow focus on decreasing the behaviour without considering how this strategy might affect other areas of the child's life.

In contrast, positive behaviour support seeks to increase the child's quality of life and focuses on positive strategies such as teaching new skills and making changes in the child's environment. Positive behaviour support promotes the values of choice, respect and inclusion and uses improvement in quality of life not only as a strategy but also as a measure of success.

In order to support a child with severe learning disabilities whose behaviour is described as challenging, it is essential to develop a positive behaviour support plan, as part of an overall joined up care plan. This plan should be drawn up in partnership with the child's family and all who know the child well. The plan is then implemented across all settings.

## Developing a positive behaviour support plan

A positive behaviour support plan is a practical tool that sets out how the child will be supported, based on an understanding of the child's needs, to ensure a consistent approach across all settings.

The key components of the behaviour support plan (BSP) are:

1.  Input from all those who know and support the child including family, school, other professionals, short break staff (key stakeholders).

2.  Functional assessment of the behaviour(s).

3. A proactive plan (how to support the child in ways that minimise the likelihood of challenging behaviour occurring).

4. A reactive plan (how to support the child safely when challenging behaviour does occur).

5. A review process (including what is learned from when the reactive plan is used, and any revisions that are required to the BSP).

Each of these key elements is now outlined in more detail.

# Input from those who support the child

The behaviour support plan must be comprehensive and holistic – therefore input from all the key stakeholders is essential. Gathering their input for the plan is beneficial for both the quality and breadth of information, but also from the joint ownership of the plan and commitment to implement it.

A behaviour support plan may already be in place – or there may be different elements of it being used by different services. If this is the case, take the opportunity to review what is in place, to see whether things have changed, whether disparate plans can be amalgamated or whether existing elements can be built upon.

If no behaviour support plan is in place, identify a lead person to coordinate its development and draw together information from all the key stakeholders. Remember that the child's family will be key partners in this work, and they will have a rich source of information to draw upon, as well as contact with other stakeholders. Input from the local educational psychologist and the behaviour support team (for example, clinical psychologist/behaviour nurse) is also advisable as well as the child's school, specific autism service if there is one in the area and the Disabled Children's team if the child is known to them. If the child is under the care of a speech and language therapist, their involvement is also useful to share levels of communication available to the child and possible alternative or augmentative communication methods, should these be appropriate.

---

**Information to be included in a behaviour support plan**

- The aims of the behaviour support plan.

- A description of the challenging behaviour.

- A description of who is at risk and why.

- A list of what recording is being done.

- The function(s) that the behaviour appears to serve.

- Potential triggers for the behaviour.

continued

---

- Proactive plan including a 'likes list' of activities that the child finds enjoyable (example of Proactive 'green' plan at the end of this chapter).

- A description of 'early warning signs' and the action that should be taken to support the child when these signs are observed (example of Active 'amber' plan at the end of this chapter).

- Reactive plan (example of a Reactive 'red' plan at the end of this chapter).

- Post incident support (example of Post-Reactive 'blue' plan at the end of this chapter) .

- A record of who contributed to and is in agreement with the behaviour support plan.

- A record of how often the plan is to be formally reviewed.

Adapted from *Challenging Behaviour – Supporting Change (Using a functional assessment to understand challenging behaviour and identify ways of supporting behaviour change)*, Mark Addison, Copyright Challenging Behaviour Foundation.

## Functional assessment of the behaviour(s)

A functional assessment is a process where information is gathered to help understand the possible causes of the behaviour for the individual – what needs are met for them by the behaviour.

A functional assessment is usually carried out by a psychologist or a behaviour support specialist, in partnership with those who know the child well, and will involve gathering and recording information.

Behaviour described as challenging can appear to be 'out of the blue'. In fact, a great deal is known about behaviour, including how it is learned and reinforced, and its purposes or 'reasons'.

Children behave in ways that others find challenging **for a reason** (in other words, it *serves a function* for them), and because **it works**. The challenge is to identify the reason/function for the behaviour, address it and at the same time provide the child with other ways to get the need met.

It is important to understand that for children with severe learning disabilities whose behaviour is described as challenging, the behaviour is highly unlikely to be a deliberate attempt by the child to harm or annoy others. Rather challenging behaviour is a way of communicating an unmet need.

It could be an indication of pain or a physical health need. It is essential to ensure that physical health needs are investigated and addressed.

The functions of behaviour are usually grouped into four main categories (see box).

## Functions of behaviour

The purpose of behaviour can be described in four broad categories:

- **Social attention:** It is not bad to want attention from others, however, for a variety of reasons, e.g. limited communication skills, some children may learn that behaviour in a particular way is a reliable way of attracting others' attention even if it is negative.

- **Tangibles:** Here it is the desire for certain things, e.g. food, favourite toy etc. which provides the motivation for the behaviour. Again it is not bad to want these things. If you are hungry, it makes sense to try to get something to eat. The problem arises when a child learns to act inappropriately to get these things.

- **Escape:** Whilst some children crave attention, for others being left alone is the ideal situation. These children may display behaviour that others find challenging to avoid situations, activities or people that they do not like or do not find rewarding.

- **Sensory:** Sometimes behaviour is internally rewarding. A child may behave in a particular way because of the sensation (e.g. rocking back and forth), because it is stimulating (e.g. 'twiddling' a piece of string) or because of the way it sounds (e.g. grinding their teeth). These behaviours may appear pointless, annoying or distressing to the observer. However, for the child themselves, the behaviours may serve the function of helping them cope with uncomfortable negative feelings such as boredom or anxiety.

Adapted from *Challenging Behaviour – Supporting Change (Using a functional assessment to understand challenging behaviour and identify ways of supporting behaviour change)*, Mark Addison, Copyright Challenging Behaviour Foundation.

# A proactive plan

A proactive behaviour support plan is a wide ranging and comprehensive plan that encompasses all aspects of the child's life, is based on information from the functional assessment and clearly sets out proactive strategies (i.e. how the child should be supported across all settings to minimise the risk of challenging behaviour being displayed).

## Examples of proactive strategies

- **Identifying triggers:** The vast majority of triggers are modifiable to a great or lesser degree. Even when this isn't the case, knowing what the triggers are can help you avoid them, or introduce the child to them in a more gradual way.

- **Teaching replacement skills:** Teaching a child a new skill, e.g. to indicate they have had enough of an activity, can help to reduce challenging behaviour as it provides the child with an alternative to using challenging behaviour to get their needs met.

- **Interaction styles:** It can be helpful to use a particular interaction style at certain times, for example, consistently being calm, firm, humorous or praising may help to reduce challenging behaviour.

- **Environmental changes:** Environmental modifications can reduce the impact of incidents when they do occur. For example, if a child throws objects you can limit the number of objects that can be thrown and ensure that the available objects are less likely to cause injury. If a young person pulls hair you can tie your hair back or wear a hat. If a child breaks windows you can have toughened glass fitted.

- **Rewards:** Rewarding children's good behaviour through the use of praise or a preferred object can be very helpful. However, it is very important that the child generally has things in their life that they enjoy. Activities that the child enjoys are an essential part of a proactive plan.

- **Routine and structure:** For children with learning disabilities who may have very limited concepts of time and great difficulties adapting to change, routine can be extremely important. A predictable routine can minimise the potential for unnecessary anxiety and associated challenging behaviour.

- **Boundaries:** It is important that children are helped to distinguish between culturally acceptable and unacceptable behaviour, e.g. taking food from other people's plates is not acceptable.

- **Support:** Whether it is practical support such as short breaks or emotional support to ease the pressure, parents should be supported to access the services they are entitled to. Paid staff should receive appropriate training, supervision and emotional support.

Adapted from *Challenging Behaviour – Supporting Change (Using a functional assessment to understand challenging behaviour and identify ways of supporting behaviour change)*, Mark Addison, Copyright Challenging Behaviour Foundation.

A proactive positive behaviour support plan, with multi-stakeholder input and implementation can deliver good outcomes for the child and those who provide him/her with care and support.

# A reactive plan

A reactive plan is also based on the functional assessment and is an agreed way to respond when challenging behaviour is displayed. In the past, the emphasis has been more on reactive plans (for example, how to physically restrain a child who is self-injuring) than on proactive plans (intervening much earlier to avoid the challenging behaviour occurring).

However, a good reactive plan should identify the early warning signs, so that you are intervening as early as possible. Early warning signs are likely to be individual to each child but may include vocalisations (for example, high-pitched scream), gestures (such as waving arm) and observable behaviours (such as shutting doors and curtains).

The reactive plan will identify a range of actions to take, which will always be ordered from the least restrictive and intrusive intervention being implemented initially, with more restrictive interventions only used as a last resort.

## Examples of reactive strategies

- **Not responding to, or ignoring the behaviour:** This doesn't mean that you have to ignore the child entirely. It may simply mean that you stop correcting the child, or giving them what they want as a direct response to their behaviour. Not responding should only be used alongside strategies that teach the child to get their needs met in another way.

- **Giving reminders:** If you are trying to teach someone new skills to replace challenging behaviour, then they may need reminders of what you want them to do instead.

- **Distraction:** Distraction, e.g. use of humour, a change of face, the offer of a preferred object, can be a good way to diffuse challenging behaviour.

- **Giving the child what they want:** If you know what the child wants it is sometimes best to give it to them! Whilst this may not provide the best long-term solution, it may help avoid an immediate crisis. If you do give in, do it sooner rather than later, as you may be teaching the child to be more persistent with their challenging behaviour.

- **Withdrawal:** Depending on the circumstances and the age of the child, withdrawing yourself from the situation, e.g. leaving the room, may be the safest option, and may even help the child calm down quicker than if you were there.

- **Physical interventions:** Physical interventions should only be considered as a last resort, and only when non-physical intervention options have been exhausted. Physical interventions and medication that is used solely to calm children down, are generally not considered a good long-term solution.

Adapted from *Challenging Behaviour – Supporting Change (Using a functional assessment to understand challenging behaviour and identify ways of supporting behaviour change)*, Mark Addison, Copyright Challenging Behaviour Foundation.

A key element that should be built into the reactive plan is a process to record and review how often the reactive plan is used.

**Note:** Current joint guidance from the Department for Education and Department of Health *Guidance on the use of restrictive physical interventions for staff working with children and adults who display extreme behaviour in association with learning disability and/or autistic spectrum disorders* (2002) is currently being revised. The revised guidance will be available on the CDC website as soon as it has been published.

## A review process

It is good practice to carefully consider what lessons can be learned if the reactive plan has to be implemented, and to identify any emerging patterns or themes (which may also require a review of the proactive plan), and to do this in partnership with parents and other key stakeholders. It is important to create a culture in which all stakeholders can openly discuss how behaviour is managed and reflect and learn from experiences.

Further input from a Behaviour Analyst or behaviour support team (who can do a more thorough behavioural analysis) should be sought, should the behaviour not show substantial improvement within the review period set in the behaviour support plan.

A behaviour support plan should be a 'living document' that is regularly updated and reviewed. Reviewing processes and requirements are outlined more fully in Chapter 13.

## Checklist for developing and implementing a positive behaviour support plan

Developing a comprehensive behaviour support plan in partnership with all who know the child well can lead to significant improvements in the child and family's quality of life, opportunities and inclusion, as well as a reduction in challenging behaviour. This checklist is a tool for monitoring progress.

☐ Information has been gathered from the child's family and all who know the child well.

☐ There is a clear description of the challenging behaviour(s).

☐ The events, times, and situations that predict both the occurrence and non-occurrence of challenging behaviour have been identified.

☐ One or more educated guesses about why the behaviour is happening have been developed.

☐ There are more proactive than reactive strategies in the PBS plan.

☐ The child is being taught new skills.

☐ Appropriate behaviour is being reinforced.

☐ The environment has been changed to remove triggers.

☐ Everyone is working together. The PBS plan is used across settings e.g. home, school and short breaks centre.

☐ The PBS plan is regularly reviewed and updated.

☐ An observable reduction in challenging behaviour has been recorded.

☐ The child's quality of life has improved.

# Organisational approach to positive behaviour support

Training, policies and record keeping should promote and support the implementation of positive behaviour support across the service. However, it is important to ensure that these elements are translated into an individually tailored approach that achieves positive outcomes for every child and their family. While individual services can have a significant impact through PBS approaches, developing these as part of a wider strategic multi-agency approach with other stakeholders can increase local capacity to meet the needs of all children.

## Good practice example

In Salford, Greater Manchester, the Local Safeguarding Children Board (LSCB) has recently launched a policy on the use of restrictive physical interventions for children with learning disabilities and autism. This policy is part of an overall strategy aimed at promoting positive behaviour support and ensuring consistent practice between services where restrictive physical interventions are deemed necessary. This response is the result of Salford's interpretation of *Guidance for Restrictive Physical Interventions – How to provide safe services for people with learning disabilities and Autistic Spectrum Disorders* issued by The Department of Health and Department for Education and Skills in July 2002. This guidance clearly spells out the need for strategic implementation and coordination. It states that 'good practice in the use of physical interventions is properly coordinated with other procedures designed to protect vulnerable people. These will include …local Area Child Protection Committees' (p. 31) .

The message being sent out to all agencies is that they should consider challenging behaviour itself to be a unique safeguarding issue that affects this population of children and young people. This strategy has high level support within the city and is reflected in the work schemes of the Children and Young People's Trust Board (CYPTB) as well as the LSCB. Parents have been involved in the development of this strategy initially through the policy task group and later through the Challenging Behaviour Strategy Group.

continued

This group is chaired by an Assistant Director from children's services and reports back to the CYTPB and LSCB. Key stakeholders from health and education are represented along with service commissioners, trainers and practitioners. Parental scrutiny and questioning is seen as one of the key ways through which good practice can be developed and sustained in the long term.

Salford is attempting to foster a culture of openness and transparency that can enable services to reflect, learn and improve. A common approach is ensured through shared reporting and recording protocols. Support to front line practitioners has come through a strategic approach to training which recognises the differing needs of practitioners in education, health and social care. Practitioners from all services are able to access a web page with links to local and national support and attend groups to discuss individual children or explore common issues in responding to children with complex needs. There are firm links and parallel practices with adult services in the city which enable smoother transition arrangements for young people entering adulthood.

More detailed information about functional assessment and proactive and reactive plans is available from the Challenging Behaviour Foundation Information sheet *Challenging Behaviour – Supporting Change (Using a functional assessment to understand challenging behaviour and identify ways of supporting behaviour change)* and the accompanying DVD *'Challenging Behaviour – Supporting Change.*

## Example 1: **Behaviour Support Plan for John**

With thanks to Andy Fenwick, Alternative Response. Copyright Challenging Behaviour Foundation

**Written on:** XX/XX/XX        **Written by:** Mary (mother) & Ms Smith (teacher)
**To be reviewed:** the last Wednesday of every month

## PROACTIVE ('Green')

The Green Proactive phase is where John is feeling mostly calm and relaxed and is able to engage positively with you in a meaningful way. It is best to try and support John to stay in this phase as much as possible.

| Support | Behaviours |
|---|---|
| • When you approach John always smile at him.<br><br>• Ensure that John stays in good health.<br><br>• Ensure that John has the opportunity to do some physical exercise at least once a day.<br><br>• Give John regular positive feedback by saying, 'Great John, you're doing really well' and giving him the thumbs up sign.<br><br>• Support John to use his Communication Board to understand what is happening in his day, use his countdown calendar to show when important events will happen.<br><br>• John likes to keep busy with activities. It may be useful to have a morning and afternoon list of activities.<br><br>• Agree with John what his responsibilities are at school (e.g. taking the register to the office) and at home (e.g. sorting the recycling/washing clothes) and give him lots of praise when he completes these tasks.<br><br>• Allow enough time for John to receive and process what has been said.<br><br>• Avoid saying 'No', try to use a positive phrase, for example instead of, 'No you can't take those keys' say 'Those keys belong there, shall we go and look at your pictures'. | • John may be smiling and laughing and this will be at a low volume and pitch.<br><br>• John's posture will be upright with his head held high.<br><br>• John will have frequent eye contact with other people.<br><br>• John will initiate communication and respond when you ask or tell him something.<br><br>• John will cooperate and enjoy activities you ask him to take part in, he will also invite you to take part in his activities.<br><br>• John will sit down in a room with other people and remain calm; he may show you his pictures and other objects.<br><br>• The pace of John's movements will be slow and relaxed.<br><br>• John likes having a list of things he needs to do throughout the day; he will be more calm and relaxed if he has a list. |

## ACTIVE ('Amber')

The Amber Active phase is where John may be starting to feel anxious or distressed and there is a chance that he may need to challenge you in some way. Here we need to take quick action to support John to return to the Green Proactive phase as quickly as possible to prevent behavioural escalation.

| Support | Behaviours |
|---|---|
| • Stay as calm as possible and use a calm reassuring voice when you communicate with John. Try not to raise your voice or say 'No' to John. <br><br>• Try to distract John by offering him an activity, drink or object that he really likes, for example looking at pictures of lorries, forklift trucks etc. You can also try singing John's favourite songs. If this is successful then redirect John away from the initial trigger for his anxiety. <br><br>• If there is something specific that is bothering John, support him to move away from it to a different area. <br><br>• If a particular question or topic is making John anxious then don't repeat or push the topic, distract John and come back to it later. <br><br>• Consider whether John may be in pain (e.g. urine infection, toothache, ear infection, constipation etc.). <br><br>• John will usually expect a task to be completed in a particular sequence – for example when using the washing machine he knows that he puts in the detergent, sets the programme and then presses the start button. (Attempting to do this in a different order will cause confusion and anxiety. If you need to perform a task in a different way, wait until he is engaged in a different activity and then do this yourself.) <br><br>• If John spills or drops something, do not laugh at him as he is likely to do this behaviour more. Either distract him while another person discreetly tidies up or encourage him to move away and then simply clean up yourself without any fuss. <br><br>• John can become anxious when you remind him about changing his continence pad. Consider supporting John with one of his favourite activities before and after the change. | • John may stop smiling or laughing and put his head down or look away. Note John also uses this to say 'No'. <br><br>• John may also start to laugh or giggle more, get a glint in his eye. His laughter will be high pitched and may increase in volume. <br><br>• John's movements may become more restless and faster. John's posture will be less upright and his shoulders will be slumped. <br><br>• John may say to you, 'Go away' or 'Leave me alone'. <br><br>• John may become tearful, ask or sign for home, Mummy, Daddy or Jessica. <br><br>• John's communication will decrease and he may not respond to requests; he will sometimes ignore some of his support workers completely. <br><br>• John may pack his bags and put them and teddy by the front door, he will also stand there. <br><br>• John may start to touch his ears or poke objects into them, he may also poke his nose with a finger until it bleeds. This may be an indicator that he is in pain. <br><br>• Less likely to collaborate and cooperate with you, will not have personal care, breakfast or engage with planned activities. <br><br>• John may start to pick up or play with keys or pull his hair. |

## REACTIVE ('Red')

The Red Reactive phase is where challenging behaviour actually occurs and we need to do something quickly to achieve safe and rapid control over the situation to prevent unnecessary distress and injury.

| Support | Behaviours |
|---|---|
| • Stay as calm as possible and communicate with a soft reassuring voice.<br><br>• Don't raise your voice or say 'No'.<br><br>• One person should take the lead in talking to John with a second person available for support if needed, but not distracting John from the lead person.<br><br>• Keep your communication to a minimum and only say what you really need John to hear; support this by using signing and pictures.<br><br>• Encourage other people to move to a different area and give John lots of space.<br><br>• If there are loose objects available that may be thrown, try to move these out of the area.<br><br>• Reassure John; tell him that he will be okay and that you are going to help him.<br><br>• Quickly distract John by offering him his favourite object, snack or activity. Use a different means of distraction every time to keep it exciting enough to appeal to John. | • John's face may turn red and will be more tense.<br><br>• John may be crying.<br><br>• The pace of John's walking and movements becomes much quicker and more urgent.<br><br>• John's vocalisations will be much higher pitched.<br><br>• John's nose may be running and he rubs his face with his hand.<br><br>• John may start to tear paper or clothing.<br><br>• John may start to spit.<br><br>• John may start to push people.<br><br>• John may push or overturn objects, for example his bed.<br><br>• John may take off his shoes and throw them. |

# POST-REACTIVE ('Blue')

The final Blue Post-reactive phase is when the incident is over and John is starting to recover and become calm and relaxed again. We still need to be careful here as there is a risk of behaviour escalating again quickly.

| Support | Behaviours |
|---|---|
| • Continue to reassure John that he is okay and give him lots of positive feedback that he is doing really well. Make sure John has enough space to move around and avoid giving him too much information.<br><br>• If you know that a particular question, topic or person was the trigger for John's anxiety and behaviour then avoid further exposure to this until you are sure that John has fully recovered from the incident.<br><br>• John needs at least 30 minutes for recovery.<br><br>• When you are sure John is fully recovered from the incident ensure you do the following:<br><br>  1. Check that everyone involved in the incident is okay and treat any physical injuries as appropriate/required.<br><br>  2. Debrief everyone involved as soon as possible and check people are okay.<br><br>  3. Inform key people (teachers, other family members).<br><br>  4. Record on ABC Chart. | • John's eye contact with you will increase.<br><br>• John's body posture will become more upright, his face will relax and return to normal colour and he will start to smile again.<br><br>• John's communication will increase and become more effective. |

## Example 2:  BARNARDO'S Sunrise Project

*Behaviour Management Plan* **BMP**

**Name**
Fred Bloggs

**Positives (what they are good at and what they like)**

Having pictures from the internet
Round things, rubber gloves, moving toys
Soft play and highly active play
Responds well to reminders of good behaviour (from staff or family)
Group games
Playing in the garden (go-karts)

**Triggers (common situations which have led to problems in the past)**

Fred has more awareness of his feelings. Has been receiving relationship/sex education at school (according to carer).
Particular members of staff.
If Fred is displaying hyperactive behaviour.

**Behaviours (behaviours displayed)**

Inappropriate touching (smacking or pinching bottoms)
Inappropriate language ('I love you')
Running around (hyperactive) and becoming over excited.

**Modifications to the Environment or Routines (what we can do to prevent problems from arising)**

Buddy Fred up with appropriate staff (someone he does not target) – a male where possible.

When Fred is in a receptive mood, remind Fred not to pinch bottoms at the beginning of sessions. Do not provide this reminder if Fred is in a hyperactive mood. However if he does display the physical touching behaviour, explain to Fred it is not appropriate.

If he asks for a massage in sensory room, agree to give a hand massage only, but do not prolong the activity beyond where necessary.

Do not encourage rough play or too much physical contact. 30 minutes before club ends Fred does not go into the soft play room or take part in exciting activities but encouraged to listen quietly to music in the sensory room.

Encourage high-fives, not hugs. Keep to firm boundaries.

Give Fred appropriate tasks to do during the day, e.g. helping with drinks. Encourage him to help clean up at the end. If he says 'I love you,' respond 'I like you too,' and distract to another activity.

**Must be completed and appended to the young person's All About Me**
To be used when child needs Restrictive Interventions

---

**WHITE LODGE
BEHAVIOUR STRATEGIES PLAN**

**Child's Name: A C**                                    DOB:  xxxxx

**AGE: 12**

---

**Pen Picture:**

**Physical Description**

I am quite a stocky young man and very strong, I do not know my own strength.

**Diagnosis**

I have a diagnosis of Autism.

**Characteristics**

I am fun loving and energetic. On domiciliary sessions I love being at White Lodge where I can swim, play and watch videos. I feel safest in the nursery. I like my own space at times and have been known to lock myself into rooms and others out if given the opportunity. I have a very good aim when throwing objects.

I very much enjoy routine and structure, but I am learning to cope with changes.

**Language**

I have limited verbal skills but I am generally able to make myself understood, this is improving but I do mimic a lot of what I have heard and re-enact situations that have caused me anxiety. Sometimes I talk too fast and people find this hard to understand. When I am starting to get angry I may swear.

---

**Staffing Levels**

I require 2 staff at all times who have positive options training.

| Scenario | Strategy |
|---|---|
| I may punch, kick, bite, head butt, throw objects or use items as a weapon. | Distraction does not work. Staff should place themselves out of the line of fire and wait A out. Do not use language or eye contact. A needs time to process his thoughts. |
| I can find transition difficult especially when I am particularly enjoying something. | Staff should wait outside the room/pool area providing they have latched the door open. They must remain vigilant. |
| I may leave the pool and then get agitated and become verbally and physically aggressive. | A generally will then calm down/return to the nursery. If necessary requesting him to get dressed should wait until this time. |
| I might want time alone. I may gently, at first, try to push you out of the room and then lock you out.<br><br>Or | CAS staff have been asked to lock their rooms at the end of the days. Staff should check this has happened. Staff should make sure they have the central key to enable them to return into Nursery should they need to. A must be observed through the window. Do not speak to A. |
| I may run to another room (generally CAS) and lock myself in. | If A attempts to initiate a hug staff should be wary. Whilst A can be a loving young man he is unable to balance his emotions and his hug can turn to physical aggression. Hugs can feel like restraint! |
| I will sometimes initiate a cuddle, but then head butt staff. | Staff should turn side on and place arm across shoulder but not apply any pressure. Disengage as quickly as possible. |
| I may become agitated in the car. | A is generally calmed with Disney or Abba songs. A prefers to use the same route on all his journeys; however from time to time this may be difficult due to road closures and ongoing work in the Woking area. A sits behind the passenger seat and the escort behind the driver. A may try to kick the driver if agitated by a change in route. Driver should be aware of their position in relation to A. Escorting staff may need to block A's movements until the car can pull over. |

Sometimes all of the above can cause me to become exceedingly distressed, which will result in me becoming very physical towards children and staff, and as a result I may unintentionally hurt myself too. I do not self harm and generally am self protecting.

White Lodge
**centre**

**Name of young person: A C**   **DOB:** xxxx   **Service:** Domiciliary

| Description of behaviour | Situation in which behaviour occurs | Injuries or potential harm | Who is at risk | Early intervention | Planned Restrictive physical intervention (if any) | Risk level reduced to acceptable level (yes or no) |
|---|---|---|---|---|---|---|
| Biting | Times of Transition | Teeth marks/ breaks to skin | Peers | See attached behaviour strategies plan | If A is unable to calm then a Medium positive options hold (previous level 2) sitting on a chair or against a wall (if possible) will be needed. Staff will need to protect A's head as he can move his head backwards and forwards very quickly. | No. **This may make A more agitated and should only be used while making area safe for others in the vicinity if necessary.** |
| Kicking | | | Staff | | | |
| Spitting | | | Members of the public | | | |
| Punching | General anxiety | Bruises | | | | |
| Throwing objects | | | | | | |
| Head butting | | | | | | |
| Two or more of the above are apparent in each episode | | | | | **If A drops to floor disengage immediately** | |

**Names of those preparing risk assessment: XXXX XXXX and XXXX XXXX**

Signatures:   Service Co-ordinator : _____   Date _____

Parent: _____   Date: _____

Review Date: March 20XX or sooner if physical intervention used

# Behaviour Management Plan

Name: Paul                           Date: 12-10-XX

**Topography of Behaviours:** (Describe what the behaviour looks/sounds like.)

- Pushing other children
- Hitting other children
- Kicking other children
- Throwing objects at other children
- Throwing objects across classroom
- Spitting – either at other children or onto table or floor
- Holding other children in a strangle hold
- Screaming

Review 16-03-XX Behaviours described now seldom seen

**Trigger Behaviours:** (Describe common behaviours/situations which are known to have led to Positive Handling being required. When is such behaviour likely to occur?)

- Looking for a reaction from either the child concerned or an adult
- Attempting to control the situation e.g. Screaming because he doesn't want people to sing

**Preferred Supportive Strategies:** (Other ways of C.A.L.M. ing such behaviours. Describe strategies that, where and when possible, should be attempted before positive handling techniques are used.)

- Use of the 'informational no'
- Withdraw Paul from situation and use a sandtimer or internal counting to 'sit' him out. Do not give any eye contact or verbal interaction
- Symbol support eg. Drink, computer
- Social story – 'Good hands'
- Ignore screaming and carry on regardless – Paul will calm after a little while and even enjoy what he was initially protesting about

**Preferred Handling Strategies:** (Describe preferred staff responses/holds)

Not applicable

**Action to be taken after incident**

Quickly praise compliance and offer reward

# BEHAVIOUR SUPPORT PROGRAMME (Level 2)
### (including Risk and Hazard Assessment)

NAME OF PUPIL   AB   AGE ..16 . . . . . CLASS. . 15 . .

**BRIEF DESCRIPTION OF TYPE OF BEHAVIOUR DISPLAYED**

AB has learning difficulties and persistent challenging behaviours and requires small group tuition with frequent opportunities for 1:1 attention.

AB can be cooperative particularly when he is engaged in an activity he enjoys. However, he is frequently becoming less cooperative and then may become physically aggressive, particularly when he does not want to participate in an activity or task set or if he needs moving on from an unsafe context, and will sit down on the floor and may attempt to kick, pinch or bite staff when they get too close to him.

The intention of this support plan will be to deal with the occasions on which AB becomes non-attentive, disruptive or uncooperative. His overall social and communication skills will be targeted through his PSHCE and language targets that are delivered on a daily basis across the curriculum.

AB is not easily drawn into normal class and school activities and when he is, it is very much on his terms. He requires much encouragement and prompting and behaviours may occur several times a day and inhibit many of his activities. He appears to have little concept of consequences and a reward system has had little effect on his behaviour. Although he will ignore requests from the teacher or staff member in charge he will occasionally immediately comply with the same request given by another adult.

**TRIGGERS TO BEHAVIOUR (and the risk of that behaviour occurring)**

AB does not respond to confrontation and therefore being told 'no' may be a trigger to his inappropriate behaviour.

He can become unsettled at particular times of the day and if this happens he should be clearly communicated with and his PECS book should be used to encourage him to choose where to go or to be shown where to go. The priority is to re-engage AB in an alternative activity through distraction and motivation. Although there are triggers to AB's behaviour, often he becomes distressed and may begin certain behaviours without warning.

**WHO OR WHAT IS AT RISK (if appropriate)**

AB is a risk to himself as he may carry out destructive activities. Members of staff engaged in keeping AB on task and engaged in learning are at risk if they adopt confrontational or unnecessarily physical interventions.

**Solutions:**

AB does not respond well to physical closeness of adults when he is anxious, so it is important to give him the space he needs and use a non-confrontational approach whenever possible until he calms down. He will seek out physical attention if he wants it, by reaching for your hand and then he can be encouraged to move to an area outside the classroom in order to calm down.

Once calmed, AB should be encouraged to return to the task/activity in hand and to continue to work at his workstation (the implementation of TEACCH strategies help to provide structure to AB's day).

He should be encouraged to undertake the task set using the full range of strategies, praise, reward, 'well done AB...' etc. This may involve offering a reward for completing a task such as using a favourite toy/activity.

When AB shows signs of becoming agitated he may respond to being spoken to softly by a familiar adult and using his PECS book be taken to a quieter area of the class to complete his work.

Increase AB's self-esteem and sense of worth by:

- Give him special jobs to do, not as a reward but as part of his agreed behaviour management. Only forbid him to do these jobs if he has misbehaved **immediately** beforehand. Do not use the jobs as a threat to ensure compliance – it does not work!

- Avoid confrontation; AB gets very uncooperative during changes of activity i.e. clearing up times. Avoid this by asking him to go on an errand out of the classroom before the tidying up begins. It does work to ask him to help with the tidying (small area e.g. his table).

- If he has been good, tell visitors to the classroom and allow him to go and tell other members of staff.

- Make a big thing of writing in his home book to tell his Dad/Carer how good he has been.

- When asking AB to do something give him a choice, i.e. 'You have a choice AB – either you can do this with us or you will have to.....'

- If he refuses or ignores your request, ask another member of staff to repeat what you have said to him.

- If all this fails then ask another member of staff to take him off for an activity as specified below. Other activities may be substituted where appropriate.

- When he rejoins the group, welcome him back and praise him for whatever he has been doing.

- If he does become violent in any way immediately send for another member of staff and allow them to deal with it.

## PERTINENT STRATEGIES FOR MANAGEMENT OF THE BEHAVIOUR

- Speak calmly but firmly to AB, letting him know what is expected from him through speech and signing.

- Reinforce good behaviour with positive comments and rewards.

- If he exhibits challenging behaviour that threatens to injure a member of staff or a pupil, first warn him, but if he continues, move him to a different area (see physical intervention, below).

- Once into a safe environment AB will need non-confrontational calming before returning to class.

- Use a range of strategies to distract and calm him, but if necessary remain at a safe distance from him unless for health and safety reasons it is necessary to intervene.

- Although he will ignore requests from the teacher or staff member in charge he will occasionally immediately comply with the same request given by another adult.

*If AB's behaviour becomes more challenging to others or property then the following procedure must be followed:*

- *Inform the Dept Coordinator ASAP.*

- *Ask AB to leave the room to calm down in a quiet area.*

- *If necessary indicate for an alternative member of staff to ask him to leave the classroom with them (this may be acceptable to AB and diffuses the situation).*

- *If support is not immediately available and AB becomes aggressive, remove peers away leaving a member of staff to observe him.*

## 2. USE OF PHYSICAL INTERVENTION (SCIP techniques to be used and by whom)

As a last resort a one-person or two-person escort may be used to support and escort AB to a safe area (the school hall, playground or field) where he can be calmed and allowed time to burn off some energy before returning to class.

SCIP Physical interventions to be used by trained class staff/SMT.

PARENTAL AGREEMENT (Signature) .......................................................................

Signed ...................................................................................... (Class teacher)

Signed.............................................................................. (Head of Department)

Signed...........................................................................(Behaviour Coordinator)

*Review date  May 20XX*

# Risk assessment to support inclusion

This section considers how risk assessments can be used positively to support inclusion. Risk assessments ensure that children can be included safely and any risks minimised. Many of the risks cannot be removed completely, but it is possible to manage them. Effective risk management will form the basis of ensuring that disabled children and young people who have behaviour that challenges are included in both specialist and universal services.

Risk assessment is part of managing risk. Risk assessments should cover activities that take place within the usual service or activity building, visits or trips away from the base, as well as the home of the child or carer if the service is delivered there.

The purpose of risk management for staff and carers is to ensure:

- that tasks are carried out in the safest possible way

- that any risk to staff and carers is minimised.

The purpose of risk management for children and young people is to ensure:

- that they are not exposed to unacceptable risks

- that they can take part and enjoy all the activities of the service or setting.

# The elements in risk management

- Risk refers to the possibility of a situation occurring that would involve exposure to danger or a hazard, that is, the possibility of something harmful happening.

- Risk is a combination of the **likelihood** of something harmful happening and the **seriousness** of the potential injury.

- A hazard is less likely to cause harm if certain controls are in place. Controls are the steps taken either to eliminate the hazard or reduce the associated risk to an acceptably low level.

- Risk is managed by **assessing it**, avoiding it if it is unnecessary and reducing it to a level which is 'reasonably practicable'.

- When considering what is **'reasonably practicable'** the needs of both the child and staff should be taken into account.

- **Reasonably practicable**, as defined by the Health and Safety Executive (HSE), means *'an employee has satisfied his/her duty if he/she can show that any further preventative steps would be grossly disproportionate to the further benefit which would accrue from their introduction' (HSE 1992, p.8).*

- A key element in any risk management strategy is **safeguarding**. Risk assessments should cover issues relating to safeguarding, for example, a restrictive physical intervention may be required when the positive behaviour strategies as outlined in the positive behaviour plan have not worked. The assessment as to whether a restrictive intervention should be included in the positive behaviour plan must balance both the child's right to be kept safe with the right to be treated with dignity.

In order to manage risk, all services will need to:

- clarify who is responsible for carrying out risk assessments

- detail the training required to carry out risk assessments

- ensure all those delivering activity/service are familiar with the risk assessment

- develop the procedures and paperwork required to carry out risk assessments

- agree on arrangements to monitor and review all risk assessments on a regular basis.

While services may draw in professionals from other agencies to help with risk assessments in specialist areas, it is the responsibility of the service to ensure that risk assessments are in place in relation to the service being provided and the setting in which it is occurring. For example, a youth club would not be expected to undertake the risk assessment for a child or young person who may require a restrictive physical intervention without specialist input. However, it is the management group for that youth club, not the professionals undertaking it, that are responsible for ensuring a risk assessment is in place, that youth club staff carry out their responsibilities as laid out in the risk assessment and that the risk assessment is regularly reviewed and updated. It is important for services to remember that a risk assessment must be carried out for a child or young person in relation to each of the settings they attend as the potential risks and hazards are likely to be different.

## Addressing fears about managing risk

Staff may have a number of concerns about the risks involved to both children and staff in including disabled children who have behaviour that challenges in their service. These include the fear that they or the child may be hurt, that they will be blamed if something goes wrong, and whether they have adequate insurance and training. These anxieties can be minimised if all relevant areas of risk have been included in the risk assessment, that adequate steps have been taken to minimise them and if all actions are 'reasonably practicable'. It is also important to bear in mind that it is the employer who would be held responsible if something went wrong and that liability only falls on individual staff members or carers if they have not carried out the task in accordance with the child's risk assessment, their training and the child's positive behaviour support plan.

## 'Think safety'

All staff working with children should have an awareness of health and safety issues and how to assess and minimise risk.

Good practice in this area of work indicates that risk assessment and risk management should not rely solely on health and safety officers. Assessments and policies should be written in a way that all staff can understand. The forms and how to assess a new situation should be written in plain English rather than in health and safety jargon.

Training staff in risk assessment is about training staff to think 'safety' rather than training staff to complete risk assessment forms. This will mean that, whatever situation staff find themselves in, they will feel confident at looking at the situation, identifying the potential risks and managing them appropriately.

## Use of equipment

If a child or young person who has behaviour that challenges also requires moving and handling, the controls identified in the risk assessment may recommend the use of equipment. Although often useful, equipment is not always the solution to every moving and handling situation. In principle, equipment should always encourage and maximise the child's or young person's independence rather than increasing dependency. Where appropriate equipment is used, staff must be trained in its usage.

Not all pieces of equipment are large and expensive; there are small pieces of equipment that are relatively inexpensive and easy to store such as handling belts. Services need to liaise with the occupational therapists already working with the child to identify ways of loaning or obtaining equipment so that the cost of the equipment does not become a barrier to the child accessing the service.

Equipment must never be used as a way of controlling a child's behaviour, for example strapping a child into a wheelchair or car seat so that he/she cannot run off or cannot self-harm. Department for Education guidance on the use of restrictive physical interventions (DES, DH 2002) is currently being updated. The updated guidance will cover best practice and mechanical restraint.

Positive behaviour support plans are critical to ensuring that staff are confident about how to support a child in ways that minimise the likelihood of challenging behaviour occurring but also address how to support the child safely and protect their dignity when challenging behaviour does occur.

## The general and the specific

Risk assessments will cover general situations as well as situations and tasks that are specific to each child and how they need to be supported. Once a service has received information about a child (described in Chapter 5) the risks specific to that child need to be identified. A positive behaviour support plan can help staff identify the additional needs of a child (which may include moving and handling or giving medicines) and clarify the safety measures that need to be in place.

Risk assessments on supporting a child or young person who has behaviour that challenges are likely to be both general and specific. A service will need a general risk assessment on the sensitivity of the environment and sensory considerations – a checklist of the kinds of things to consider is given in Chapter 13. A risk assessment relating to an individual child or young person who may have specific sensory issues and support needs will also be required. While the service is responsible for ensuring that risk assessments are in place, this is best done with the input of a professional such as a member of staff from the behaviour support team or autism specific team, who will carry out the risk assessment together with service staff. However, the responsibility for ensuring that it is followed is with the service provider not the professional.

At the end of this chapter is an example of a risk assessment from White Lodge School in Chertsey. This is part of the child's 'All About Me' information.

Risk assessments on moving and handling are also likely to be both general (for example, applicable to all the children who use wheelchairs) as well as specific (relate to the particular needs of an individual child). As with behaviour that challenges, the service is responsible for ensuring that the risk assessments are in place but these should be carried out jointly with a specialist who knows the child's moving and handling needs and can train the staff.

The following is an example from Abbey Court School in Rainham of a risk assessment for an educational visit, looking at the risk posed by the young person's behaviour and the potential moving and handling needs.

**FORM RA003**

## DETAILED RISK ASSESSMENT

| Risk assessment location: | Abbey Court School, Rainham | | |
|---|---|---|---|
| Task being assessed: | his behaviour re. 'Runner' on Ed Visits | | |
| Assessor's name: | JB | Date: | 4.4.XX |

| **HAZARD / HARM POTENTIAL** | **SEVERITY 1 to 6** | **FREQUENCY 1 to 6** | **RISK RATING (auto calc.)** |
|---|---|---|---|
| 1 He may 'run' when on an educational visit and is unaware of dangers – injury/fatality | | | |
| 2 He may 'run' when on an educational visit and get lost – safeguarding issues | | | |
| 3 | | | |
| 4 | | | |
| 5 | | | |
| 6 | | | |
| 7 | | | |
| RISK POTENTIAL | 4 | 4 | 16 |

| **FACTORS THAT INCREASE RISK** |
|---|
| 1 Staff unaware of his behaviours |
| 2 Staff distracted from providing individual support |
| 3 Staff unfamiliar with his behaviour support programme and IEP |
| 4 Untrained staff (Manual handling and PROACT-SCIPr-UK) |
| 5 |
| 6 |

| 7 | | | | |
|---|---|---|---|---|
| 8 | | | | |
| | RISK POTENTIAL | 5 | 4 | 20 |

| | **CONTROLS NEEDED TO REDUCE POTENTIAL** |
|---|---|
| 1 | Class staff are aware of his current behaviour support programme |
| 2 | Individual member of staff identified as 1:1 support for him on visits and free from distraction with additional member of staff immediately available on request to support should it be needed |
| 3 | Any staff providing 1:1 support to be trained in PROACT-SCIPr-UK ® |
| 4 | Manual handling assessment |
| 5 | Any staff providing 1:1 support to be trained in Manual Handling procedures |
| 6 | Member of staff with minimum of emergency aid training to be on the Educational Visit |
| 7 | |
| 8 | |

| | REVISED SCORE IF CONTROLS PUT IN PLACE | 3 | 3 | 9 |
|---|---|---|---|---|

| | **OTHER MEASURES RECOMMENDED** |
|---|---|
| 1 | Risk assessment of all educational visits carried out by class teacher/ approved by trained Educational Visits coordinator |
| 2 | Adhere to Abbey Court local visits by foot risk assessment and Ed Visits policy |
| 3 | Include reference to this risk assessment on his IEP |
| | REVIEW DATE:    Sep-XX |

There is specific legislation and guidance that covers the management of risk in this area. The regulations state that risk assessments should cover:

- the lifting task: why is it required, are there alternatives?
- the child or young person's weight, needs and abilities
- the physical environment
- the individual capacity of the person doing the lifting.

There is also specific legislation and guidance on the regular maintenance and checking of equipment. It is the responsibility of the service to ensure that regular checks are carried out in accordance with these requirements including equipment in the child's own home if that is where the service is provided.

If a service is using equipment – such as mobile hoists – specific risk assessments may need to be carried out on the use of this equipment by a qualified person – such as a physiotherapist or occupational therapist.

## Specific policies

There are specific regulations and guidance for certain areas and they are likely to be covered in the employer's health and safety policy and guidance. These areas are:

- storage of medicines
- Control of Substances Hazardous to Health Regulations 2002 (COSHH)
- clinical waste
- infection control
- fire and evacuation procedures.

**Risk Assessments**

## 2b. Pool Risk Assessment

| |
|---|
| I need this help to get changed...I am independent and need privacy post swim. Close supervision must be maintained. Following my swim I may want to return to the Nursery before getting dry and dressed. I may need support with dressing, but can do it myself if given enough time. Let me do as much as possible myself as dressing me is an invasion of my personal space. Give me verbal prompts to get dressed. |
| I need this help to access the shower and then the poolside... Supervision and verbal encouragement to have a shower but do not enforce this |
| I get into the water by...independently using the steps |
| **I need this level of help in the water** 1:1 supervision |

| I use: | no arm bands....if I am in water that is not out of my depth like the White Lodge swimming pool. |
|---|---|

| |
|---|
| I am unable to swim but I am very confident in water. Be aware I like to try and get poolside staff very wet and enjoy trying to catch them out. I also like it when they throw water back at me and I like to tell you 'missed' – staff should get water close to A but not so the majority of the water lands on him. Staff in the pool should be aware that I will try to initiate rough and tumble games in the water but I am unaware of my own strength and I don't know when to stop. Please discourage rough and tumble games by distancing yourself or remind me to be gentle. I like to pull the pool cover when session over. |
| I get out of the pool by...myself independently using the steps – I may be reluctant to do this and need time for transition. Ask me if I want to watch videos rather than telling me the session has finished, I will then come out in my own time. |
| I get back to the change room by...walking independently but I may prefer to dress in the Nursery area. Encourage me to cover myself with a towel. I can manage to dress myself but need support. |
| **Whenever I use a swimming pool my carers need to be aware of the following risks...** Wet surfaces and bare feet a combination of which increases the likelihood of slipping Unclothed bodies and hard surfaces which increase the likelihood of injury if slips or trips occur Collision with other swimmers leading to injury/distress Shallow water areas where diving/jumping by unskilled persons may lead to injuries of a serious nature A **will use nets, mop and brooms housed in the pool area as weapons** **Level of risk involved – Medium** **Risks can be reduced by:** **Removing mop, broom, and nets from pool area once A is in the water.** Ensure staff trained in the use of the recovery board Remind A not to run and to use steps into the pool and to be aware of others. Ensure A is supervised at all times |
| I need one staff/volunteers poolside when I swim |

## 2c. Transport Risk Assessment

**Please note that from the 18th Sept 06 for children under 135 cms in height (who are also under 12 years of age) a booster seat (or appropriate car seat) must be used to conform with legislation**

**Car Assessment**

| |
|---|
| Help me get into the car by...I can get in independently |
| Once in the car I sit in...normal car seat behind front passenger seat. Escorting staff to sit behind driver.<br><br>I may have a bag with me, do not touch this bag unless I ask you to. I may choose to put my belongings in the boot of your car or I may place them on the car seat next to me. |
| The seatbelt I use is...standard three point seat belt. Be aware I can undo this so need supervision. Please help me to fasten seat belt if I ask you.<br><br>**Staff must ensure that child safety locks are switched to on when transporting A. Risk assess boot and car prior to picking up A. A likes to find objects and will use them inappropriately.** |
| These things help to distract me if I become bored or upset...I enjoy travelling in the car. I like Abba and Disney music. Little toys can distract me.<br><br>I like to follow the same routes and become upset when there is a detour.<br><br>If I become cross I may spit or throw things.<br><br>I may try to kick the driver.<br><br>Ignoring me can help if safe to do so.<br><br>If I am causing a risk pull the car over until I have calmed down. |

## References used in this chapter

Department of Health and Department for Education and Skills (2002) *Guidance for Restrictive Physical Interventions: How to Provide Safe Services for People with Learning Disabilities and Autistic Spectrum Disorder.*

# 9. Communication

## Why communication?

Communication is fundamentally important to all children and young people. It is an essential component of their overall development and can be the gateway to other aspects of learning, such as literacy. Communication allows interaction with others, is the mechanism by which young people can make and share their decisions and influence their lives. It allows children and young people greater independence and inclusion in their communities and enables them to express their opinions and feelings. Challenging behaviour is often seen as the way in which individuals can communicate their feelings, wants and needs when access to other communication is not available to them or temporarily breaks down.

## What do we mean by communication?

At its most basic, communication involves the exchange of information between two or more people. This can take place verbally using and understanding the words and sentences spoken or non-verbally using signs, symbols or other communication aids. Lots can be communicated without words.

Developing language and communication is the most complex skill we ever learn and involves the following areas:

- Understanding of language, whether spoken or sign language, including:
  - understanding and using 'higher order' language skills, such as inferencing, reasoning and use of jokes, idioms and sarcasm.

- Talking or expressive language, including:
  - development of vocabulary, grammar and narrative skills to communicate with others
  - using clear speech to talk to others or use of signs for children who have no speech.

- Using social interaction skills, including:
  - understanding and use of non-verbal communication, such as eye contact, taking conversational turns, interpreting facial expressions and body language.

The majority of children with severe learning disabilities and those on the autistic spectrum will have communication needs. Although they communicate about the same things as other people – their wants, needs, interests and feelings – the way in which they develop and use their communication is likely to be more idiosyncratic, and at times ambiguous, than typically developing children. Development is likely to be slow and, may not follow typical developmental milestones.

The idea of communicative intent is particularly important as a young person may use noise, gestures and words, but may not be intending to communicate with others. Some young people may be very late in developing verbal language or may never use words to communicate; depending on other means of non-verbal communication. However, communication is a skill that can be learned and developed and it is important to continue supporting communication skills in all children and young people.

## The adult's role

Adults have a fundamental role to play in supporting the communication of children around them. Typically developing children rely on good quality and quantity of interaction to develop their language and communication skills.

This role is equally important when working with children and young people who have severe learning difficulties and autistic spectrum disorders. The conversational partners for these children play a crucial role in supporting and interpreting their attempts to communicate. There can be massive variation between individuals in both the extent to which messages are intentional and the support they need from communication partners, but there is no doubt of the difference a supportive communication partner can make to effective communication.

Wherever possible, adults working with these children should:

- be skilled in interpreting their communication in order to support interaction and avoid frustration

- offer a range of opportunities for youngsters to interact with others wherever possible

- be able to encourage and facilitate development of communication skills, based on their own skills and in collaboration with specialists, such as speech and language therapists where appropriate.

## Communication needs

Children and young people on the autistic spectrum and those with severe learning difficulties may have a range of communication needs; outlined below.

### Difficulties with understanding

It can be incredibly frustrating to spend a lot of time not understanding the words that are being said or the situations in which you find yourself, particularly if there is a lack of insight from others that this is the case. In addition, there may be implications in terms of not having needs met or finding additional challenges because of a lack of understanding.

Difficulties with understanding may include the following:

- Children may struggle to understand certain words or concepts. For example, concepts of time are particularly difficult for children to understand, so giving instructions or information about what is going to happen in the future may be challenging; youngsters may interpret the information as what is going to happen in the here and now. This type of misunderstanding can cause frustrations and resulting behaviour.

- They may have a limited vocabulary and may struggle to learn new words. For children on the autistic spectrum, this may be alongside a particularly rich vocabulary in a specific area of interest, which might present a deceptive picture of their overall understanding.

- They may struggle to process large amounts of information, so will not be able to follow long or complex instructions. Children can appear to lose interest in what is being said or may take a long time to respond while they are trying to process information. They may also appear very passive in such situations or again, may become frustrated with 'information overload'. Finding themselves in trouble for 'not listening' can also be extremely frustrating as they may be making great efforts to follow what is being said.

- They may struggle with understanding sequences of events, such as stories or step-by-step instructions, unable to hold the sequence in their heads. Children on the autistic spectrum can struggle to see the 'big picture' and may give too much emphasis to small details that can impact on their overall understanding.

**Watch out for**

- Children who respond to just part of an instruction or who 'echo' back to you some or all of what has been said – it's a good indication they haven't understood.

- Children who seem to have immediately forgotten what has been said, who take a long time to respond or who seem 'lost'.

- Children who don't seem to understand certain words or ideas or get cross because the situation isn't what they expected.

- Children who begin to get agitated when they are expected to listen in certain situations – it can be a precursor to challenging behaviour.

- Children who are passive and who can become angry or aggressive if they are encouraged to listen – sometimes there is just too much information so they choose to 'opt out'.

- Anxiety in youngsters who are struggling to understand.

**What can help?**

- Ensuring you have good attention before giving information.

- Giving instructions in short 'chunks', one step at a time.

- Giving time for youngsters to process information fully.

- Taking care about the words and amount of language used.

- Checking understanding.

- Giving information in a one-to-one situation can support careful listening and enable the adult to adapt the complexity and pace of their talking.

- Visual support, such as using simple signs or symbols or using visual timetables to help children understand ideas outside of the here and now can be incredibly helpful in reducing anxiety.

## Taking things literally

Many children on the autistic spectrum do not have the ability to infer meaning and will take what is being said very literally. This can also apply to some degree to children with severe learning difficulties, though they are more likely to not understand at all, than consistently interpret literally. They may take common sayings very literally and might struggle with more abstract words, which, though very common, are difficult for these children to understand, such as abstract nouns, being kind and telling the truth.

**Watch out for**

- Children who respond literally to certain phrases; for example pulling socks up when told to 'pull your socks up'. It can be quite frightening for children when these idioms are used, which they don't understand and can lead to poor or challenging behaviours. For example, using idioms like it's 'raining cats and dogs' or uncle Jim is going to 'drop in' soon.

- Children who seem to be struggling following certain instructions, for example 'line up' or 'fold your arms' in school is difficult when taken literally.

- Children who can appear rude or disobedient, for example responding to 'can you open the door' with 'yes'.

- Children who respond literally to sarcasm – 'I love that noise you make, Jack'.

**What can help?**

- Being aware of literal and inferred language.

- Avoid metaphors and colloquialism.

- Avoid ambiguity.

- Being sure to explain when non-literal language is being used.

Some of this may need to be specifically taught.

## Difficulties with talking/expressive language

- Children may struggle with vocabulary development, which means they may take a long time to learn new vocabulary or forget new words and names for things. It can make talking seem quite disjointed or full of words that have little content, such as 'that', 'this', 'thing' etc. Children can experience some frustration when they want to make their needs known, but they don't have the right words to explain or listeners are struggling to follow their train of thought.

- Children may struggle to combine words and sentences in a way that makes sense, either through lack of organisation or through poor grammar or language structures. Again, this can make them difficult to understand and can lead to frustrations.

- Some children, may learn in rote phrases or longer strings of language, which they may use without any real understanding. They may have well formed sentences that they appear to use reasonably well, though they might not use them in a truly communicative way for interaction with other people.

- Some children may have good language, but have unclear speech, which can make them difficult to understand.

- Some children, particularly those on the autistic spectrum can speak without expression, using a fairly monotone way of communicating.

**Watch out for**

- Children who use lots of empty words or a reduced vocabulary.

- Lots of false starts when attempting to communicate, which can lead to frustration.

- Repetition of phrases, echoing or copying elements of what they have heard, which often isn't used for communication and can indicate poor understanding, too.

- Children who talk a lot, but when you listen carefully don't make too much sense or what they are saying is a repetition of a TV programme or familiar story.

- Children who have unclear speech who may withdraw or become frustrated.

**What can help?**

- Using the same words in different situations and contexts can really help children to learn new words – repetition is the key.

- Visual aids can help children structure longer sentences and narratives and can help children remember words.

- Using augmentative or alternative communication, such as simple signs can help those children whose speech is very unclear as well as those with limited language.

# Difficulties with social interaction

Many children, have difficulties with social interaction skills. This may be because they have poor language skills or may be because, despite reasonable language, they are unable to use these skills socially. Some children can struggle to stick to a topic of conversation or may pursue their own particular areas of interest, despite clear inattention or disinterest from conversational partners. Difficulties can span across both verbal use of language and non-verbal skills, such as understanding non-verbal communication and cues. Difficulties with social interaction can lead to real misunderstandings and can result in social isolation for many youngsters, both of which can be linked with challenging behaviours.

**Watch out for**

- Children that are socially awkward who may have limited use of facial expression, poor turn taking and eye contact. These children may struggle to understand the significance of these skills and struggle to 'read' others, as well as showing difficulties using these skills.

- Children who continue a conversation, in spite of the cues received from their conversational partners.

- Inappropriate responses that can appear rude, dismissive or overly formal with peers. They can seem not to be interested or care about the people they interact with.

- Limited use of facial expression and intonation when talking and listening.

- Poor awareness of the needs of the listener in terms of their interest and also in terms of what they know already; they may talk like they assume shared knowledge.

- A lack of communicative intent.

- Children who are isolated socially.

**What can help?**

- Giving guidance about social situations can be helpful, though it's important that they are not seen as being too rigid as this too can cause difficulties.

- Interventions, such as social groups or social stories approaches can be useful.

- Following the child's lead and encouraging less rigidity in their interactions can be helpful.

# General good practice

All children and young people are very different in the way they communicate. Levels of understanding and talking for youngsters on the autistic spectrum and with severe learning difficulties can vary widely. Because of this, probably the most important factor when considering communication is to have some knowledge of the way in which children and young people can communicate and the levels at which they understand.

Knowledge of both these areas can help, particularly with proactive behaviour strategies, but can also ensure any reactive behaviour strategies are pitched at a level that children can access. Breakdown in communication can be a source of challenging behaviour. Effective communication with children, at whatever level and through whatever means, is important to manage challenging behaviours. Additionally children may be using challenging behaviours to communicate their wants and needs.

There are a number of resources and tools that can help gain an understanding of communication levels. First and foremost is to gather information from the young person, parents and carers as highlighted in Chapter 5. In addition, materials can be used to track children's communication development and can be a good way to gather and share information with parents (see References at the end of the chapter).

**Information on the child** The admission form or information that services ask parents to complete must always include details about the child's communication, including triggers and indicators of stress. This information should be recorded as part of the child's positive behaviour plan and shared with all the staff who support that child.

**Communication passports** A good way to collect information on communication to ensure it is used in the widest possible way is through a **personal communication passport**. For children who have severe learning disability or children with autism who communicate in an individual way, using a communication passport to understand their communication and behaviour can be very helpful. Some will have a detailed communication passport, written and developed by their school or by a speech and language therapist. For others, a more simplified 'one-sheet' version may suffice. Communication passports include information about the child, how they communicate and how to interpret their communication. An example of a detailed communication passport (names of the service and family have been changed) is shown at the end of this chapter.

If a child does not have a communication passport such as the one above, a more simple passport can be developed to ensure that all staff understand the child's non-verbal communicative behaviours. There is an example of one developed by a child's parents in partnership with the Early Years service at Torfield, prior to her transferring to the school, shown at the end of this chapter.

Another option is 'All About Me' books. These are used in some settings in a similar way to communication passports or in others are used for young people to develop and share with people around them.

There is an example from White Lodge Centre in Chertsey, Surrey, of the communication profile section of their 'All About Me' form at the end of this chapter.

# General strategies

Some useful general strategies include:

- Have clear and consistent routines, using the same language to describe them, with clear starting and ending points to sessions or activities – this helps children feel secure and can be a good way for them to associate specific language with specific activities.

- Gain attention, using children's names and support them to develop their listening skills; finish activities on a success, rather than losing their attention along the way.

- Choices are important, though it may be useful to give two or three simple options for children to choose from if understanding is limited.

- Use visual tools, such as signs and symbols, to support understanding and talking and visual timetables to support organisation and understanding of the day's activities.

- Prepare children in advance if there is going to be a change to the usual routine – this can be done by adding a 'change' symbol to the visual timetable.

- Have visual displays of activities as a reminder and centre point for discussions.

- Be aware of the language you are using and levels of understanding of the young person.

- Give information in short chunks, with time to process information or ask for help in between.

- Ensure instructions are concise and easy to understand and where appropriate in the 'here and now', for example 'Walk please' rather than 'Could you please stop running'.

- Repeat and reinforce new ideas and information, especially new words that can be hard to learn or remember.

- Be careful with using 'higher order' language, such as idioms, inference, jokes and sarcasm.

# Communication is a skill

Communication is a skill like any other and can be developed with lots of practice. The process is much slower for these children and they often need a lot of repetition before words and ideas 'stick'. The best way to do this is through everyday activities that children are engaged in and enjoy.

- Describing their activities while they are doing them can help them attach meaning to words being spoken.

- Providing opportunities for youngsters to use communication **at their own level** can be incredibly powerful.

- Using visual support and alternative or augmentative communication can be useful in helping youngsters gain communication success.

# Interventions

A range of interventions can be used more formally to support communication development, though these are often delivered with support from a specialist such as a speech and language therapist. Examples include:

- Intensive interaction for pre-verbal children with more significant needs.

- Comic strip conversations designed for pupils on the autistic spectrum to help them understand that what people think and what people say might be different.

- Narrative approaches to support those who have language to develop more complex narrative structures.

- Approaches to support vocabulary development for children with severe learning difficulties.

- Social stories to support children with communicating in different social situations.

There are various sources of information on interventions for children and young people with communication needs. One is the Better Communication Research programme *What Works* database, developed by the Better Communication Research Programme and The Communication Trust. It includes a range of interventions, some of which are suitable for children on the autistic spectrum or with severe learning difficulties. Another source is around communication with people with the most complex needs, developed by Mencap (Goldbart and Caton 2010).

# Practical ways of working with alternative communication methods

Alternative and augmentative communication may be the most appropriate option for children, either as a temporary strategy to facilitate development or augment verbal communication or as a more permanent method of communication.

# Examples of alternative and augmentative communication

- Signing, including Makaton and Signalong.

- Low tech communication aids, such as use of communication books and symbol supported communication.

- High tech voice output communication aids (VOCA).

- Applications for tablets and smartphones.

- PECS – Picture Exchange Communication System.

- Use of photographs, pictures and symbols, such as Boardmaker or Widgit.

- Talking mats, which is a low tech communication framework using symbols.

- Applications for tablets and smartphones such as Proloquo2go enable children to talk using symbols or typed text in a natural-sounding voice that suits their age and character

(See references for more information on alternative and augmentative communication.)

## Mobile phones, tablets and apps

For some disabled children who use speech but find eye contact or listening difficult, new technology can be a real asset. Many find that they can more easily express themselves using text or picture messaging, or chat forums (aimed at and for children) when they are not required to have face to face interaction with another person. Care should always be taken around safeguarding issues, though these sites can be a useful social outlet for some children and young people.

Apps such as Proloquo2Go (for iPad, iPod Touch or iPhone) convert symbols and text into speech, which is then read aloud via the speakers. Children and young people who have difficulty communicating can choose from about 8,000 symbols or tap out a sentence and give a voice to their thoughts. Although not yet an alternative to a well-developed communication aid, they can provide some useful simple messages for young people to use.

# Training/workforce development

As communication is so fundamental to children's quality of life as well as having specific and direct links to positive behaviour, it is useful for staff to have at least a basic grounding in understanding language and communication alongside general communication strategies that can be used to support and facilitate communication development in children and young people.

The speech, language and communication framework (SLCF) is a competency based framework and a good starting point for staff to determine their own knowledge and skills in supporting the communication needs of children and young people (see www.communicationhelppoint.org.uk). It provides a profile of strengths and areas for development and signposts a range of options to support professional development in this area. For staff members who want to develop more formal skills, an award is available that staff can study as part of their professional development (see http://www.thecommunicationtrust.org.uk/schools/training-and-qualifications.aspx).

For more specialised areas of communication, such as formal signing systems, staff or carers may need additional formal training. British Sign Language (BSL) is a comprehensive language in its own right. Children using BSL to communicate will need to be supported by staff or carers who are trained in BSL. It is unusual for children with severe learning difficulties or ASD to use these systems unless they also have other sensory deficits such as a significant hearing loss. They are likely to use less complex signing systems, such as Makaton or Signalong.

If children use Picture Exchange Communication System (PECS) staff or carers may require some specific training to ensure that it is put in place and supported properly. However, some other communication methods, such as symbol communication, Makaton or Signalong, can be learnt by staff or carers alongside the child with a minimum amount of formal off-the-job training.

## References and further information

### Materials to track communication development

Early support developmental journals http://www.councilfordisabledchildren.org.uk/early-support/resources/developmental-journals

Universally Speaking – typical language development booklets from 0 – 18 (The Communication Trust) http://www.thecommunicationtrust.org.uk/resources/resources/resources-for-practitioners/universally-speaking.aspx

### Information on interventions

What Works – database of evidenced interventions for SLCN (The Communication Trust) https://www.thecommunicationtrust.org.uk/schools/what-works.aspx

Goldbart, J and Caton, S (2010) *Communication and people with the most complex needs: What works and why this is essential* http://www.mencap.org.uk/sites/default/files/documents/2010-12/Comms_guide_dec_10.pdf

### More information on alternative and augmentative communication

ACE centres for low and high tech AAC http://acecentre.org.uk
Apps for AAC www.appsforaac.net/

Makaton – signing and symbols http://makaton.org/
PECS – Picture Exchange Communication System http://www.pecs.org.uk/

Signalong – sign supporting system http://www.signalong.org.uk/

Talking mats – symbol based method of communication http://www.talkingmats.com

### Information and training

Speech, language and communication framework:
http://www.communicationhelppoint.org.uk

Continued Professional Development Award in Speech, Language and Communication http://www.thecommunicationtrust.org.uk/schools/training-and-qualifications.aspx

**TORFIELD SCHOOL PASSPORT**
Information from Early Years and Parents prior to starting at Torfield

**All About Me:** Maisie
**DOB:** 14th August 20XX

INSERT PHOTO

**My Family and other significant people** – Elizabeth (mother) John (father)

| | |
|---|---|
| **Medical Needs**<br>I am not taking any medication at the moment<br>I am allergic to Penicillin<br>I have had a few absences. Flickering lights and the computer may have an effect on me. After an absence I will "jump" out of them. Please record any absences observed as I am going to see the doctor in a months time | **Toileting**<br>I am potty trained<br>I am not yet using the toilet<br>I will go by myself<br>I can ask for help if I cannot manage clothing |
| **Things I like**<br>I like "Bear" and I take him everywhere with me.<br>I like playing with baby dolls<br>I like sand and water play<br>I like looking at books | **Things that upset me**<br>If I lose Bear I will become very distressed<br>Loud noises upset me especially vacuums and hand dryers<br>I get anxious about unknown objects.<br>I don't like changes to my routine but I am starting to respond to symbols warning me of the change |
| **Food – likes**<br>I like fruit. My favourite are bananas.<br>I like Cheese<br><br>**Dislike**<br>I don't like vegetables<br><br>I will keep eating until everything is gone. I don't know when I am full and when to stop eating.<br>I can feed myself with a spoon and fork | **Sensory**<br>I am very sensitive to textures- I don't like labels in my clothes or wearing socks and shoes.<br>I don't like messy activities and getting my hands dirty.<br>I find it hard to sit on a chair to listen to a story. I like to sit on a cushion.<br>I am very sensitive to sounds and I don't like noisy places |
| **How I communicate**<br>I often hold an adults hand and take them to what I want<br>I can ask for things I want<br>I have learnt phrases from my favourite tv programmes and computer games which I often say when asked a question.<br>I often say "no thank you" when I don't want to do something | **What I understand**<br>I can understand short phrases<br>I respond well to Makaton signs and symbols<br>I am able to follow "now and then" symbols<br>I can use photo symbols to choose a toy |
| **Things that make me calm**<br>Giving me a toy will often distract me and I will calm down<br>I like to sit next to an adult and listen to a story<br>I like to cuddle my bear | **What I might do when I am anxious**<br>I may go to a corner and hide<br>I may make a shocked face<br>I may drop to the floor<br>I often scream and run away |

**Other Notes**
I have a high pain threshold. If I fall over I will not respond much and I am unable to tell an adult that I have hurt myself.

**Pre School visits**
**Nursery visit date:** visit Tues 6th September 9;30
**Home visit date:** Thursday 8th September 1:30

**School start date:** 12th September

**Proposed travel arrangements** – Taxi

**Children and Young People**

# All About Me

Place photo here

## My Name is: A B

## All About Me: A B

**Contents / Checklist**
**Sections 1a, 1b, 4a, 4b and 4c must be completed in all cases.**

1. General
      1a. General Information ...................................................Completed
      1b. Involved Practitioners..............................................Completed
      1c. Care and Social Needs ............................................Completed
      1d. Communication Profile............................................Completed
      1e. Behaviour Support Plan...........................................Completed
      1f. Mealtime Guidelines...............................................Completed
      1g. Bed Time Routine ................................................ Not Relevant

2. Risk Assessments
      2a. Manual Handling ................................................ Not Relevant
      2b. Swimming.............................................................Completed
      2c. Transport..............................................................Completed

3. Health
      3a. Health Care Plan....................................................Completed
      3b. Epilepsy Treatment Plan ....................................... Not Relevant
      3c. Rectal Diazepam .................................................. Not Relevant
      3d. Buccal Midazolam ............................................... Not Relevant
      3e. Gastrostomy / nasogastric tube ........................... Not Relevant
      3f. Epipen.................................................................. Not Relevant
      3g. Oxygen ............................................................... Not Relevant
      3h. Suctioning............................................................ Not Relevant

4. Consent
      4a. Consent................................................................Completed
      4b. Permissions.........................................................Completed
      4c. Signature Sheet....................................................Completed

**Each content description must show either completed or not relevant**

## 1. General Information

### 1a. General Information – Me

| I like to be called: | A | Nationality: | British |
|---|---|---|---|
| Date of birth: | 11th November XXXX | Religion: | C of E |
| Nature of disability: Autistic Spectrum Disorder | | Ethnic origin: | White British |
| Name and date of birth of siblings: XX | | Language(s) spoken at home: English | |
| Home address: | | Name and address of school: | |
| Home tel: | | School tel: | |

### 1a. General Information – Parents / Guardians

| | 1 | 2 |
|---|---|---|
| Name: | | |
| Relationship to child: | Mother | |
| Email: | | |
| Place of work: | | |
| Tel. (mobile): | | |
| Tel. (mobile): | | |

### 1a. General Information – White Lodge

| Aspects of White Lodge used: Domiciliary | **Prime contact: XXXX XXXX** |
|---|---|

Through using White Lodge, I would like to experience the following benefits or changes:

1. Burn off some of my energy
2. Experience new activities and those I enjoy

Through using White Lodge my family would like to experience the following benefits or changes:

1. Spending extra time with the other children
2. Catching up with household chores

## 1a. General Information – Emergency Contacts

|  | Contact 1 | Contact 2 |
|---|---|---|
| Name: |  |  |
| Relationship to child: |  |  |
| Telephone number: |  |  |
| Mobile number: |  |  |
| Address: |  |  |

## 1a. General Information – People who may not have contact with Me

| Name:<br><br>Relationship to child: | There is no one who may not have contact with me |
|---|---|

## 1b. General Information – Practitioners Working With Us/People to invite to meetings

| GP: | Dr R | Social Worker: |  |
|---|---|---|---|
| Address: |  | Address: |  |
| Tel number: |  | Tel number: |  |
| Email: |  | Email: |  |
| Community Nurse | N/A | Health Visitor: |  |
| Address: |  | Address: |  |
| Tel number: |  | Tel number: |  |

## 1c. Care and Social Needs – General Mobility

Encourage me to… stay close and hold hands when we are out and about as I have a very limited sense of danger and might run off.

The hand I favour is… either.

## 1c. Care and Social Needs – Personal Care

Help me with toileting by… reminding me to go to the toilet, or taking me when I indicate I need to go. I am otherwise independent.

Encourage me to… wash my hands, show me what to do and help me with soap.

Help me with washing by… Giving me constant verbal prompts and visual indicators. I like having a bath. I am reluctant to bath on Mondays/Tuesdays and Sundays. These are busy days for me. I have an odour so need to keep clean. If I refuse to bath I have a wash. I am not keen on showers.

Encourage me to… do as much as I can. I need encouragement to wash my hands. I need help to put the soap on and visual actions showing me what to do.

Help me with dressing by… I am very independent but may need help to get my clothes the right way round. I need help to put my socks on and tie my laces. I have Velcro shoes which I do myself.

Encourage me to… do as much as I can. Get my shoes on the right feet.

Help me with brushing my hair / teeth… I don't like my hair brushed so mum keeps it short. I prefer to brush my hair myself but need help to do it properly. I will tolerate my teeth being brushed and like to do some myself. When I have head lice mum puts the lotion on while I'm asleep or I won't tolerate it.

Encourage me to… try and brush my teeth.

## 1c. Care and Social Needs – Relationships

I relate to other children… I enjoy their company on my terms; I need a lot of space to myself and see invasion of my space as an attack in which I need to defend myself. I like playing with other children but sometimes I can become too rough and excitable and I might push or hit them. I need time and space on my own to calm down.

Time with other children needs to be limited and built on and carers need to be alert to my changing mood.

I relate to other adults… well on my terms. I enjoy playing with adults, particularly being chased by them, and I can be very affectionate. If I am angry or upset, I might hit and kick the adults around me. When I get excited by a game I may start to get aggressive – tell me to be gentle – staff should give me the opportunity to calm down.

## 1c. Care and Social Needs – Religious / Cultural Observation

I would like to enjoy as many varied experiences as possible

(Festivals I can participate in) I celebrate… everything!

(Festivals I cannot participate in) I do not celebrate… there is nothing I may not celebrate

I shouldn't… N/A

## 1c. Care and Social Needs – Fears / Anxieties

I am fearful of … loud noises (though I make plenty of my own!) and I might cover my ears. Otherwise I have a very limited sense of danger and I'm not scared of anything!

I become anxious at times of transition and need time and space to move on. Use now and next PECS cards to help with this. I may throw PECS cards if angry.

I make a fuss about spiders but will kill them. I am fearful of dogs.

You can help me by… reassuring me and offering me time and space.

Carers should not offer a cuddle, even though he may seek this. A may interpret the contact as an intrusion into his personal space and feel the need to defend himself. Should A look for a cuddle, rather than rebuff A, staff should turn side on and place arm across shoulder but not apply any pressure. Disengage as quickly as possible.

## 1c. Care and Social Needs – Activities

I really enjoy… running and chasing, being outside, parks, walking, soft play, imaginative play with small figures, playing catch and football, riding a bike, watching nursery rhyme videos, wildlife, bugs, anything to do with sharks and penguins, painting / art. I am really into Disney Films. I like things on DVD as I like rewinding them and re-enacting scenes from the films.

If playing chase A will need time to calm down from the activity and understand the game is over before moving onto the next activity.

I dislike… sitting for long periods of time and waiting, but I am getting better. I also struggle with transitions but I am also getting better with this.

I go to these clubs… N/A

## 1d. Communication Profile

I communicate by… very animated facial expressions, body posture and vocal tone – I am very expressive of how I am feeling. I have some speech which is clearer now and improving – generally I use simple sentences and phrases, and I point to what I want. I am gaining a widening vocabulary as time goes by.

I will generally use two word phrases when I am anxious/upset about something. My language at this time can be inappropriate.

When I am happy I use lots of words but tend to speak very quickly and this can be difficult for carers to understand.

I prefer you to communicate by… speech. Use basic language and use gestures to reinforce the spoken word. I respond well to PECS particularly in the form of a timetable or used when I am cross or upset.

Staff should use limited speech when I am upset, angry or there is a change of plan.

I must have access to... PECS pictures as I find them easier to understand than speech. They are a good visual reinforcement when you are asking me to do something.

## This is how I...

| Message | Method |
| --- | --- |
| Gain attention: | I will shout to you, point or pull your hand. |
| Request food or drink: | I help myself, or bring you juice and a cup. I will ask for specific things. |
| Request toilet: | Take myself to the toilet or ask. |
| Indicate Yes: | Say 'yes'. |
| Indicate No: | I say 'no' and cross my arms with my face in the air. |
| Greet you: | Say 'hi', smile or clutch and play with your arm. |
| Request help: | Say 'help', shout or take you to what I need. |
| Show illness or pain: | I might go quiet and rub where it hurts. I will say 'hurt'. I like to have a plaster for cuts. I can specify where I have pain. |
| Show anger: | I shout, spit, sit on the floor, hit and kick, and throw things. |
| Show fear: | I will say 'Aah' particularly around spiders. |
| Show happiness: | Smile and laugh. |
| Show tiredness: | I go quiet, yawn or just go to sleep. |
| Indicate choice: | I will point or take what I want. |

## 1e. Behaviour Support Plan

I may become anxious or upset if... I don't want to finish an activity I am enjoying, if I don't know what is happening, if I can't have something that I want or if I have to wait.

If I am poorly or in pain I can become anxious and upset. I express this through my behaviour.

I don't like dead ends or blocked roads. I know my routes/directions and like these stuck to. I will point in the direction I like to be driven to and from the White Lodge Centre.

I become frustrated if I am trying to communicate something and am not being understood.

| I may... | Throw things at you, hit, kick, spit, scratch and bite. |
|---|---|
| Help me by... | Ignoring me if safe to do so.<br>Give me time and space. Use PECS rather than words and do not make eye contact. |
| **Don't...** | Come into my space whilst I am still angry as I will hurt you.<br>Don't use the word No as this makes me cross. |
| I may... | Refuse to leave somewhere and sit on the floor. |
| Help me by... | Structuring my time and giving me plenty of warning in advance of transitions.<br>When it's time to go, being firm and giving me lots of prompts.<br>Giving me space and time to work through my upset. |
| **Don't...** | Surprise me with sudden transitions if they can be avoided. |
| I may... | Play with knives. I have no sense of danger. |
| Help me by... | Encouraging me to use knives appropriately and making sure I do not have open access to them.<br>Not giving me access to knives unnecessarily. |
| **Don't...** | Leave me unsupervised in the company of knives. |
| I may... | Hit, kick, scratch, bite or refuse to move if I get somewhere and it is not open. |
| Help me by... | Checking opening times before we go somewhere. |
| **Don't...** | Take me near a favourite shop or activity if it is not going to be open. |
| I may... | Throw things. I may throw glass or objects at glass. |
| Help me by... | Supervising me at all times.<br>Not allowing me access to glass objects. When I am upset remove objects from me before I throw them, where possible. |
| **Don't...** | Put yourself in the line of what I am throwing. |
| I may... | Climb and jump. This includes walls. I am very agile.<br>I will run from you if I don't want to do what you are asking. |
| Help me by... | Supervising me at all times. Give me plenty of warning before transitions. |
| **Don't...** | Take your eyes off me. |

| I may... | Lock you out of rooms. |
| --- | --- |
| Help me by... | Understanding I am looking for some time out. Ensure you have the central key to gain access if you cannot see or hear me. Providing you can hear or see me leave me be; I will unlock the door when I am ready.<br>If we are using the garden I may lock you out of the building – when working with me unlock the training room door, but do not open it, so there is a way back into the building. |
| **Don't...** | Try to stop me locking you out – I may hurt you. |
| I may... | Swear and use inappropriate language. |
| Help me by... | Understanding I am looking for some time out, giving me space and ignoring the language. |
| **Don't...** | Respond to the language in any way. |

**Staff need to be aware that A is predictably unpredictable, He will develop behaviours to adapt to strategies put in place. Staff must be ready for this.**

**NB:** Staff are advised that any form of physical intervention should be avoided with A as this is likely to escalate behaviours.

## 1f. Mealtime Guidelines – Positioning and Utensils

| I sit ... at the table sometimes . |
| --- |
| The types of cup, plate, bowl and cutlery I use are... fork and knife. I can use a knife and fork to cut but will often pick things up with my fingers. |
| To protect my clothing I use a... N/A |

## 1f. Mealtime Guidelines – Food

| My food must be... as it comes. |
| --- |
| I really like to eat... Lots. Sandwiches, crisps, apples, meat, vegetables, Yorkshire puddings, eggs, sausages, jacket potato, cucumber, spaghetti bolognaise. Scrambled, fried and boiled egg. Anything chicken based especially chicken drumsticks. Fish, grapes (green) and carrots. |
| I really like to drink... Fruit Shoots, squash, water, cartons of Ribena. |
| **I am allergic to... nothing known.** |
| I must not eat... There is nothing I cannot eat, please encourage healthy options though. |
| I dislike... milk, mashed potato, cereal, salad, plums. |

### 1f. Mealtime Guidelines – Assistance

Encourage me to… use my fork and to eat all my lunch, not just my favourite bits. Use a knife appropriately as I like to play with them.

Be aware that… I play with knives and have no sense of danger.

## 3. Health

### 3a. Health Care Plan – General Health

My general health is… ok, though I get a lot of colds and coughs. I have recurrent verrucas.

I take regular medication for… none at present.

My medication is administered by… N/A

You can help me by… N/A

**I am allergic to… nothing known.**

I take emergency medication for… N/A

### 3a. Health Care Plan – History

Illnesses I have had… Chicken Pox.

Immunisations:

| Type: | Date: |
| --- | --- |
| 1. Diptheria/Tetanus/Hib/Meningitis | 9/3/00 |
| 2. Diptheria/Tetanus/Hib/Meningitis | 6/4/00 |
| 3. Diptheria/Tetanus/Hib/Meningitis | 15/6/00 |
| 4. Measles Mumps Rubella | 14/12/00 |
| 5. | |
| 6. | |

I have been in hospital during the last two years for… I have not had any admissions. I did break my right arm in Oct 2010.

### 3a. Health Care Plan – Notify Parents/Carers of Minor Accidents/ Incidents…

When I am collected or return home.

## BELIEVE IN CHILDREN

# PERSONAL PASSPORT

For:

Name: David

D.O.B: 16.06.04

# All About Me

## What makes me special:-

- Hello, my name is David

- I am full of energy and always move around at a running pace

- I have a 'cheeky' sense of humour

- I am sensitive to some sounds and will often wear ear defenders at the Barnardo's Day Care service

## Even more Important Things:-

- I need to have boundaries and a visual timetable to help me understand the routine of the day

- If I am told something is going to happen, I need it to happen straight away or I will become agitated and upset – if I am shown a sand timer I still need it to happen 'now'

- I can sometimes become stressed and upset if I am unsure and will throw myself to the ground. I will usually calm down fairly quickly if I am spoken to clearly and given a visual cue to what is happening

## My Medical Needs:-

- I sometimes get constipated – if this happens my Mum gives me some medicine called 'Movical'

## Physical Needs:-

- I am very physically able in all areas but I have no awareness of danger and of harming myself and others

- I still wear pull ups but at the day care service. I sit on the toilet and I have done a wee (once or twice)

- I like to follow a 'routine strip' of going to the toilet and I like to flush it – occasionally I still put my hands in the toilet water

## Mealtimes:-

- I can eat by myself using all cutlery

- I have a packed lunch at nursery and enjoy a variety of foods

- I use an open cup

## Favourite Activities:-

- I love to be in the garden where I enjoy 'pretend' cooking – mixing dirt, sand, grass together to make a 'meal'

- At home I like to watch cookery programmes on the television

- I like being read to and I like to make words using letter tiles

- I can also read words

## Communication:-

- I am able to communicate both verbally and non-verbally

- My words can sometimes be difficult to understand as I have only developed my language in the last few months – if I say something and you repeat it wrong, I will tell you 'No'!

- I use a PECS book at mealtimes and I also sometimes use Makaton

## Family & Friends:-

- My Daddy is often away from home because of work – my Mummy works hard and so I spend time at Granny's house

- I like to go to my house and be with my cousins

## Barnardo's and Other Nursery/Pre-school:-

- I started at the Barnardo's day care service in November 2008. I was looked after by Sarah, Pip, Elaine and Jenny

- My friends there were my twin brother, and Sebastian, Jared, Angus, Louise, Anna and Raniyah

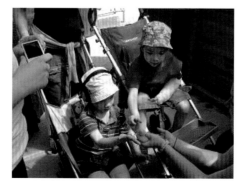

- I also went to Village House Nursery, where I was looked after by Rosie

# 10. Training

Training is an important element in successfully supporting children and young people who are on the autistic spectrum and/or have a severe learning disability. Supporting them through positive behaviour strategies that are consistent across their school and the services they use, and their home environment, is key to ensuring that children and staff remain safe and that children and young people have positive experiences.

The level of training required will depend on the type of service and the likely level of support required by the child or young person.

## Working with parents

There has been greater recognition in recent years of the importance of working in partnership with parents of children with autism and severe learning disability in order to more effectively support them in schools and services. Generally parents are the prime carers and they, not professionals, spend the most time caring for their child and so they know best how to manage their child's behaviour. Additionally, there has been increased awareness of the importance of early intervention for parents – providing them with support and training as soon as possible after diagnosis means that they learn early on how best to deal with their child's behaviour and prevent it from escalating into something more 'challenging'. Not only is such early intervention good for children and their families, but it is also a cost-effective way of supporting them as funding invested now can prevent more costly provision later on.

Below are some examples of staff, carers and parents undertaking training together on supporting positive behaviour. Learning and training alongside each other ensures consistency in the way a child's behaviour is supported and managed. It can also help to foster good relationships in the long term – again essential to positive partnership working between a child's family and the services they access.

### Example 1 – EarlyBird Programme

The EarlyBird Programme was developed by the National Autistic Society. It is a three-month programme that combines group training sessions for parents with individual home visits and video feedback. Parents have a weekly commitment to a three-hour training session or a home visit and to ongoing work with their child at home throughout the three-month programme. The programme helps parents to understand their child's autism, structure interactions in which communication skills can develop and pre-empt and deal with problem behaviours.

The aims of the EarlyBird Programme are:

- To support parents in the period between diagnosis and school placement.

- To empower parents and help them facilitate their child's social communication.

- To help parents establish good practice in handling and dealing with inappropriate behaviours at an early age.

One example of how the programme is provided is the Barnardo's Hamara Family Service in Waltham Forest, which has been offered to local parents since 2001. The Barnardo's programme is funded by Waltham Forest Children's Services although parents are referred primarily through health once the child's diagnosis has been made. Hamara then runs three programmes a year, one of which is a twilight session so that working parents can attend. Six families attend at a time and a crèche is provided for parents who need it. The service includes two Urdu speaking trainers so that they can easily accommodate the large local Urdu speaking community.

The service also run EarlyBird Plus for parents of children aged 5–8 and this programme trains staff, teachers or learning support assistants alongside parents. The upside for parents of both courses is that they feel more confident in helping their children develop communication, social and play skills and in dealing with 'unwanted' behaviour. They are also more confident in working alongside their child's school to ensure a consistent approach to meeting their child's needs.

As well as providing training to local parents, Hamara is also commissioned to deliver training to mainstream schools and Children's Centres. Local schools that have opted for specialist status around autism have asked the service to come and train all staff including midday supervisors and caretakers.

## Example 2 – Co Production

Co Production is a workshop for families and professionals developed and delivered by the Challenging Behaviour Foundation. This approach is one where all stakeholders, including family members and professionals, are considered as partners with a valued contribution to make. They jointly agree what is required, and then work together to put it in place. Key aspects of Co Production are:

- The training was co-produced by families and professionals, ensuring the content, format and terminology used was the most effective possible.

- The training model uses a Positive Behaviour Support trainer and Family Carer co-trainer delivering the training together, ensuring that 'theory' is rooted in day-to-day reality.

- Families and professionals are facilitated to work together to identify appropriate behaviour support strategies for specific individuals that can be used consistently in all settings.

The benefits of a co-production approach are that there is a greater likelihood of success: there is 'sign up' from all the partners and a holistic and consistent approach is maintained. Further information on Co Production workshops is available from the Challenging Behaviour Foundation: www.thecbf.org.uk

## Example 3 – Cygnet Core Programme

The Barnardo's Cygnet Service based in Bradford has drawn together the expertise, experience, skills and resources of young people on the autistic spectrum, parents, statutory and voluntary agencies to coordinate and support the development of the Cygnet programme. The service now has a range of programmes that provide support and training for parents and practitioners. One of these is the Core programme, which is designed for parents of children and young people aged 7–18 with an autistic spectrum condition, in response to requests from parents with 'older' children for information and support. The programme is designed to:

- increase parents' understanding of autistic spectrum conditions

- help parents develop their knowledge on how a child on the spectrum experiences the world and what drives their behaviour

- guide parents through practical strategies they can use with children

- direct parents to relevant resources

- give parents the opportunity to meet with other parents who have had similar experiences and gain support and learn from each other.

The programme is delivered over six sessions lasting three hours, which sequentially work towards behaviour management and covers a number of topics including:

- autism and diagnosis

- communication

- sensory issues

- understanding behaviour

- managing behaviour

- choice of topic decided by parents/carers.

Additional sessions include:

- supporting siblings

- puberty and sexual health.

The Core programme and others developed by Cygnet are available for purchase nationally by organisations that have skilled staff who can deliver the programme in their locality.

# Basic awareness training

Over recent years, far greater knowledge and awareness of the behaviour of children with autism and severe learning disability has developed – understanding more why their 'challenging behaviour' occurs and the strategies that can be used to better support them. Staff or carers who will be working with children and young people who have autism or learning disability should therefore have basic training on how having autism or a severe learning disability affects children and young people and how, in general, to support them.

## Example 1 – Behaviour that challenges

Torfield is a community special school in Hastings for children aged 4 to 11 with autism, language and communication and associated learning difficulties. The school also has an inclusion support service to promote the successful inclusion of children with autism and severe social communication difficulties in their mainstream primary schools and to provide opportunities for children at Torfield to experience social and curricular activities alongside their peers from mainstream schools. One of the roles of the inclusion support service is to train individuals and teams and an outline of their course is given at the end of this chapter.

## Example 2 – Cygnet Practitioner Training Programme

This programme is designed for any practitioners who either work **directly or indirectly with children on the autistic spectrum,** e.g. in schools, in long or short term residential services, CAHMS or practitioners whose work may be shorter term, e.g. in short break services. The Cygnet practitioner programme provides the tools to enable practitioners to make a difference and enhance the life chances of this group of children.

The programme is delivered over two days:

Practitioner 1 is an introductory programme that provides a description of what autism is and how the characteristics of autism are likely to be displayed while also considering parents' perspectives and family support needs.

Some practitioners find that Practitioner 1 training meets their organisational and personal development needs; others need further information and move onto Practitioner 2 training that sequentially builds on the introductory information provided in Practitioner 1 and has the following learning outcomes for participants:

- To understand children's behaviour and behaviour management frameworks used with children on the autistic spectrum.

- To be able to use behaviour management strategies and resources.

- To understand key principles of behaviour management.

More information on all Cygnet Programmes can be found at www.barnardos.org.uk/cygnet.

# Advanced training including restrictive physical interventions

Physical interventions generally occur when there is an increase in the level of risk to the child or other people. Well-targeted training will ensure that staff understand when it may be appropriate to use physical interventions as a last resort. Good training in behaviour support will explain the de-escalation, prevention and communication skills necessary for preventing behaviours that are described as challenging and emphasise avoidance of escalating situations and implementing restrictive physical interventions. Importantly, good training will also emphasise the legal framework.

In order to remain calm in times of crisis, staff and carers need to understand when it may be appropriate, proportionate and necessary to use a restrictive physical intervention, given that all alternatives have been tried and proved to be ineffective. Any training that includes the delivery of physical intervention techniques will need to be learned and will require follow-up refresher courses. The risks to a child or young person increase substantially if a technique is not performed correctly.

The cascade model for this training is not effective and training should be provided by accredited training organisations and preferably ones that are experienced in training on children and young people's issues, rather than adults. The British Institute for Learning Disabilities (BILD) www.bild.org.uk provides a number of FAQs on topics that should be covered in any training course on physical interventions. These include:

- positive values in work with children who have behaviour that challenges
- legal responsibilities of staff and protection for children and young people using the service
- physical interventions policy of the agency
- a focus on preventative approaches to behaviour management
- primary prevention; secondary prevention
- developing positive behaviour support plans
- principles of least restrictive intervention and gradient of control
- team work
- recording and monitoring.

Whichever organisation delivers the training, it is crucial that there is consistency for the child and young person and that the service uses the same technique as the child's school. This is why the process of gathering information on the child and working in partnership (Chapter 5) prior to a child starting the service is so important. Whichever training provider is commissioned, the training should be delivered by a BILD accredited training provider using an appropriate curriculum for services for children and young people. Staff and carers must be given regular opportunities to update and refresh their training. Further information on training can be found at the BILD website, www.bild.org.uk.

# Training in communication

As outlined in Chapter 9 on Communication, there are a range of augmentative communication systems – such as PECS (Picture Exchange Communication System), Makaton or Signalong – that can help some children with autism and severe learning disability to express themselves. When staff or carers are working with children who use an augmentative communication system, it will obviously be useful for them to have some training in it. Further information can be found at www.makaton.org; www.pecs.org.uk; www.signalong.org.uk

# Training in moving and handling

Some children and young people who have behaviour that challenges may also have physical impairments and therefore require support with transfer.

Many services, particularly larger ones, may undertake general training for all staff that will give them a good understanding and knowledge of the general principles around 'moving and handling'. The general training needs to be focused on 'children' rather than objects or adults and should be conducted by a trainer approved and experienced in working with children. NHS Trusts have mandatory training processes for clinical staff to ensure the safety of children requiring moving and handling. External services (The Disabled Living Foundation for example) also provide training courses in moving and handling.

Appropriate training ensures that children are always transferred using approved processes. Training in moving and handling needs to be undertaken by all staff undertaking this activity. This training cannot be 'cascaded' by one member of staff attending a course to other members of staff nor can training around one child be generalised to another child. Although it is good practice to invite parents to attend the training, parents cannot train the support staff. A risk assessment should be carried out on an individual basis for a specific child who requires moving and handling to determine the safest mode of transfer. This plan should be disseminated to all staff involved in supporting this individual.

No-one should carry out any moving and handling procedure until they have received accredited training and been deemed competent. Training should always be provided by an accredited trainer. Employers need to offer regular opportunities for staff to update their training. Training should teach safe lifting techniques whilst also highlighting lifts to avoid and the evidence base that has led to the technique being categorised as unsafe. Training needs to ensure that staff are competent and confident to perform their duties safety. The Health and Safety Executive advises that where there are high risk activities, such as people handling, then regular competency based assessment and monitoring of activities is required and should be documented. Update or refresher training should be provided when competency assessment identifies the need for further training (HSE Briefing Note). Poor skills in a particular technique may be managed by giving advice/demonstration and practice in the workplace or where there are significant issues of referral for formal training.

Generally child-specific training is carried out by a physiotherapist, occupational therapist or back care specialist. It is always preferable to use the professional already known to the child. This will mean that the training and any follow-up support will be more holistic and child-centred – rather than moving and handling being seen as an entity separated from the other aspects of the child's life; for instance a child's response to the invasion of their personal space, or the fragility/integrity of their skin.

For children who present a moving and handling risk, staff should be trained in undertaking a risk assessment prior to planning and executing moving and handling. Risk assessment helps to ensure that the safest techniques are identified and then supported through training and/or the assistance of equipment. All staff working in an environment where it may be necessary to support a child to move or transfer should have competencies in safe moving and handling practices, ensured by their employer.

Following moving and handling training for a specific child, staff should carry out a risk assessment in order to inform decisions around the safest mode of transfer and then write down the instructions on each move as part of the child's healthcare plan or as a specific moving and handling plan.

Staff will also need training on equipment used for specific children. Equipment, such as hoists and overhead tracking, must be regularly serviced and maintained. There should be an agreement as to who owns the equipment as well as who is responsible for maintaining and servicing it. This applies to equipment used in the child's home by staff and carers who may too be employed by the parents through direct payments or personal budgets. It must always be remembered that devices such as wheelchairs should not be used to prevent or control behaviour that challenges.

The 'All Wales NHS Manual Handling Training Passport and Information Scheme' contains comprehensive advice and best practice information around moving and handling and is applicable to services in England.
www.scotland.gov.uk/Resource/0040/00402969.pdf

The Scottish Government have, in partnership with Capability Scotland have produced a concise and accessible guide for workers and employers who work with children and young people with moving and handling needs – The Common Sense Approach to Moving and Handling of Disabled Children and Young People.
http://www.capability-scotland.org.uk/media/187957/movingandhandlingmobile.pdf

## Safeguarding

Training on positive behaviour strategies and restrictive physical interventions should be placed in a wider context rather than purely focusing on supporting the 'behaviour'. The other issues that should be part of this training are:

- An understanding of why children and young people who have behaviour that challenges are more vulnerable to abuse. Staff should receive training on practices that minimise the risks of abuse.

- Promoting dignity and respect in the way in which a restrictive intervention is carried out.

- Understanding the child's method of communication, particularly where this is predominantly non-verbal so that the support staff can pick up and respond appropriately when a child or young person is experiencing stress that may escalate into 'challenging' behaviour.

## Outline of Awareness Training by Torfield Inclusion Support Service

### Supporting means understanding

Behaviour challenges with children with ASD usually arise out of **anxiety**, or not understanding the **hidden rules** of social behaviour.

Discuss with the person next to you behaviours you find challenging Think about what makes a behaviour challenging to you.

### Outcomes achieved through behaviour

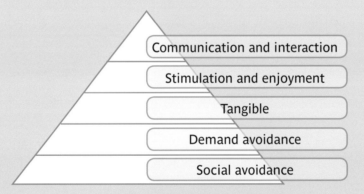

Communication and interaction

Stimulation and enjoyment

Tangible

Demand avoidance

Social avoidance

### Consider triggers for behaviour

Triggers cause the behaviours. Triggers may be due to:

- Communication difficulties

- Social interaction difficulties

- Inflexible thinking/lack of imagination

- Language – level of understanding?

- Memory – are demands too high?

- Transitions – often cause problems

- Environment as a sensory trigger

continued

**Proactive strategies to reduce anxiety**

1.  Provide consistent routines

2.  Anticipate and avoid difficult areas/events if possible

3.  Adapt the physical environment

    *   Low visual stimulation – display free, pattern free, no hanging mobiles, windows
    *   Low social stimulation – away from others, positioning
    *   Low sound stimulation – quiet voices, no loud music, maybe separate room
    *   No distracting resources – closed cupboards

4.  Provide visual support

    *   Class timetable
    *   Individual timetable
    *   Routine and surprises
    *   Sand timers
    *   Traffic lights
    *   First ....., then ......

5.  Find ways to motivate

    *   Quick rewards, 'hands-on' rewards
    *   Choice board
    *   Let's make a Deal
    *   Individual sticker charts
    *   Group or class reinforcement – 'beans'
    *   Praise may not be enough
    *   Motivation may not be intrinsic

6.  Develop social skills

    *   Social stories
    *   Social skills training – social rules
    *   SULP – Social Use of Language
    *   Role-play
    *   Puppets

7.  Assess understanding of speech and support communication through:

    *   Makaton/signing
    *   Visual supports – pictures, symbols or photos
    *   Key-word simplification
    *   Minimal speech

continued

**Being analysts**

- Structured methodical analysis

```
        ABC of Challenging Behaviour
        ┌──────────┬──────────┐
    Antecedent  Behaviour  Consequence
```

- Understand the child – why is he/she anxious?
- Consider every detail – 'hidden' triggers
- Assess risk
- Write an Individual Behaviour Plan
- Never sit back feeling satisfied. Review.

**Writing an Individual Behaviour Plan (IBP)**

- Topography of Behaviour (what it looks/sounds like)
- Triggers
- Preferred Supportive Strategies
- Preferred Handling Strategies
- Action to be taken after incident
- Date for review

**When behaviour becomes very challenging**

- Risk assessments
- Training
- Ask for help
- Know what to do and say
- Know where to take child or others
- Know what to do next

**Understand the child, understand the behaviour**

With understanding comes

- proactive prevention and management of challenges
- confidence
- control
- reduced emotional stress for you.

## References used in this chapter

HSE Human Factors Briefing Note No. 2: Competence
http://www.hse.gov.uk/humanfactors/topics/02competency.pdf

# 11. Written information

This brief chapter provides a checklist of the written information that services need to hold in order to safely include children whose behaviour challenges. The amount and detail of information gathered and stored by a service should be proportionate to the level of service that the child or young person is receiving. This means that schools are likely to hold more information on a child than a youth club attended once a week for three hours.

It is essential that information be gathered from the child's parents, other significant family members and other settings that the child attends to ensure consistency. Using information from other services also helps smaller services that do not have the staff capacity or expertise to collect all the information they may need. It is also critical to optimal transition between pre-school or nursery and school. Information should include:

- An 'All About Me' form or passport with the child or young person's likes or dislikes. Examples are given in Chapter 9.

- Contact details of family members, other key professionals involved and who to contact in an emergency.

- Information on the child's preferred method of communication – this information may form part of their Communication Passport (see Chapter 9 for more detail). It is also useful for services to have information on where staff can go to obtain additional support or resources if the child uses an alternative form of communication, such as Makaton or a symbol system.

- A care plan – this could be a single plan with specialist plans attached or as modules of that single plan. Specialist plans may include positive behaviour support plans, emergency healthcare plans etc.

- Positive behaviour support and other specialist plans – these can either be part of the main care plan or separate plans. Services may need help to write some of these. For example, assistance from a learning disability nurse and parents to write a positive behaviour support plan detailing the strategies for supporting a child or young person; or help from a physiotherapist to write a moving and handling plan. Smaller services may wish to adapt the plans written by larger services.

- Risk assessments specific to the child or young people with behaviour that challenges; these will also be specific to different settings or activities.

- Information on any regular medication that needs to be administered or verified by a medical practitioner. At the end of the chapter is an example of a letter sent out by a short breaks team in Gloucestershire to obtain information from the GP as well as the medication and diet forms used by that service.

Family Link
Jordans Brook House
North Upton Lane
Barnwood
Gloucester GL4 3TL
Fax: 01452372XXX

**Please ask for:**　　JP　　　　　　　　　　**Phone:** 01452 618XXX

**Our Ref:**　　　　JP PG/　　　　　　　　　　**Date:**

**Child's Name:**

**D.O.B:**

**Address:**

Dear GP

I am a Paediatric Nurse working for Family Link which is a service that provides short-term breaks for children with disabilities. In order to improve our practice and verify medical information, please can you send/fax a printout medical history for the above named child. I request where possible that this includes:

- The child's diagnosis and/or medical condition
- A record of illnesses and surgical procedures
- All regularly prescribed medication (please complete form enclosed, stating whether the child/young person can manage their own medication safely)
- Medical devices in use
- Immunisation record and any precautions required for safe care practice in the community

A copy of the Medical Authority Form which includes parent's consent to share information is enclosed for your reference.

A pre-paid envelope has been provided for the return of forms enclosed.

Yours sincerely
Miss XXXX XXXX
Family Link Nurse

## Prescribed Regular Medication Record

Please use **black ink** and CLEAR WRITING when filling out this document as policy. Please input CONTROLLED DRUGS onto form (MH1b) as supplied.

Child's Full Name:

Date of Birth:

Any known allergies/sensitivities:     Nil known         (Refer to child's care plan)

| Generic Medicine Name & Type (tablet, liquid etc) | Strength of Medicine | Dose Prescribed | Route of Administration | Time/s to be Given | Health Professionals Signature/Date |
|---|---|---|---|---|---|
| | | | | | |
| | | | | | |
| | | | | | |
| | | | | | |
| | | | | | |

It has/has not been agreed that the child/young person named above is able to safely self administer their own prescribed medicines.

Comments/guidance on self administration (Refer to Care Plan)

Health Professional's Signature.................................................................................     Date.........................

Other signature.................................................................................     Date.........................

Children's Centre
City Hospital Campus
Hucknall Road
Nottingham
NG5 1PB
Tel: 0115 8831XXX

# URGENT INFORMATION REGARDING MEDICATION

Re:                                                    (Child's details)

This patient was reviewed in clinic today and the following medication was started or changed:

Yours sincerely

Signature:

Print Name:

Date:

## Resource examples

Letter to GP – Gloucestershire County Council, Family Link Service

Record of Medication – Gloucestershire County Council, Family Link Service

Letter on change of medication – Nottingham Children's Hospital

# 12. Written records

It is essential that services maintain ongoing records not only to comply with regulations and standards but to ensure that they are continuing to provide a safe service for both children and staff. This chapter provides a checklist of the kinds of written records services need to hold when including children who have behaviour that challenges. Local authorities need to talk to parents who employ personal assistants using direct payments about the written records they will need to maintain.

- Services need to record the routine giving of medication. An example of the form used by the short break service in Gloucestershire is at the end of this chapter. For children who take a number of medicines at different times of the day, a single 'drug sheet' that stays with the child should be considered. This is particularly important when children are being treated with controlled drugs such as morphine.

- Services should record when medication or another form of rescue treatment is given. In cases when either an adrenaline autoinjector is used for a severe allergic reaction or Buccal Midazolam is given in case of a seizure and an ambulance is then called, the adrenaline autoinjector or syringe should be given to ambulance staff. The dose given is then recorded by the ambulance staff and relayed to the staff in the hospital emergency department.

- When an incident occurs where a child or young person potentially or actually injures themselves or others the incident must be recorded.

- Services must keep a record of when staff have received training, who provided the training and when that training is due to be updated.

- If a child uses any equipment, a record should be kept of when it is serviced and maintained. This includes ensuring that equipment in a child's own home is maintained regularly if that is where service provision takes place.

- If a child or young person cannot join in with activities because of their support needs, this should be recorded and discussed at the child's review. These records should contribute in a positive way to future service planning and ensuring that the service becomes more inclusive over time.

- As with all children, if there are child protection concerns more detailed and specific notes or records will need to be kept.

It is important to apply a principle of proportionality to the records that front-line staff are required to keep so that they are not spending an unreasonable amount of time on record keeping and away from direct contact with children and young people.

Where service provision takes place away from the service base, for example in a child's own home or the home of a short break carer, robust systems need to be in place to ensure that the written records of staff and carers are regularly added to the child's main file.

**Resource examples**

Recording chart for all medication administered – Gloucestershire County Council, Family Link Service

MH6a

# Recording Chart
# for All Medication Administered

Child's Name ................................................................

Date of Birth ................................................................

Any Known Allergies/Sensitivities............................

.........................................................................

(Use in conjunction with child/young person's individual care plan)

# Note:

Check!! Right child, Right drug, Right dose, Right time and Right Route - **BEFORE** administering **ANY** medication.

# 13. Conclusion and checklist

This publication details a process that will assist services, whether specialist or universal, to include disabled children with high support needs. The publication describes 11 areas that need to be considered in order to support children in a safe and inclusive way. The process can be used whether providing direct services or in situations where parents are the employers using direct payments or other forms of personalised budgets.

This checklist will assist the reader to consider whether or not they've considered the issues covered in the chapters; not all will be relevant to every child. The checklist should be used together with the more detailed information in earlier chapters.

## Checklist for inclusion

| Developing policies and procedures: | Yes | In part | To be developed |
|---|---|---|---|
| Has the drawing up of the policies and procedures involved managers, commissioners, front-line staff (from all agencies) and families? The process should also involve local unions and associations. | | | |
| Are they in line with the local area arrangements? | | | |
| Does your policy include information on: | | | |
| The roles and responsibilities of staff and other carers? | | | |
| The roles and responsibilities of all agencies, including funding arrangements for additional support staff? | | | |
| The training and support that staff carrying out additional tasks can expect? | | | |

| | Yes | In part | To be developed |
|---|---|---|---|
| What the service expects from families? | | | |
| Insurance or indemnity arrangements? | | | |
| Risk management, record keeping? | | | |
| Arrangements that will be in place in the case of an emergency? | | | |

| Implementing policies | Yes | In part | To be developed |
|---|---|---|---|
| Have all staff read and understood the policies and procedures? | | | |
| Is there agreement by all agencies to follow the same policies and procedures? | | | |
| Is there a process for monitoring and reviewing policies and procedures? | | | |

| Information on the child – working in partnership with the parents | Yes | In part | To be developed |
|---|---|---|---|
| Prior to starting a service with a child who has behaviour that challenges do you have a method of recording information about their disability, support needs and any medical conditions? | | | |
| Is your organisation clear about who decides how much and what information will be shared with staff? | | | |
| Are there clear principles on which this decision is made? | | | |
| Is there a timely process for passing on and receiving information when a child with high support needs moves from one service to another? | | | |
| Do staff know where to seek more information about particular conditions or how those conditions may affect a child or young person? | | | |

| | Yes | In part | To be developed |
|---|---|---|---|
| Are parents involved in drawing up positive behaviour support and other plans? | | | |
| Are staff clear when they need parental consent? | | | |
| Where consent is required from the parent, does the organisation have in place the forms to obtain that consent in writing? | | | |

| Partnership with the child or young person | Yes | In part | To be developed |
|---|---|---|---|
| Does your organisation work in a way that ensures all children and young people participate in decisions that affect their lives? | | | |
| If the child or young person uses non-verbal communication is the meaning of their non-verbal communication recorded and shared with all staff (for example through the use of a communication passport)? | | | |
| Does your organisation work in a way that ensures the dignity and privacy of children with high support needs is respected at all times? | | | |
| Are staff clear about the law on consent as it relates to children and young people? | | | |

| Plans | Yes | In part | To be developed |
|---|---|---|---|
| Does each child or young person have in place a plan/plans that cover positive behaviour support, communication, health needs, moving and handling and intimate care – as appropriate? | | | |
| Was the plan/s drawn up with the involvement of all staff who hold key information about the child's health needs as well as the parents? | | | |

| | Yes | In part | To be developed |
|---|---|---|---|
| Does the plan cover: | | | |
| The specific procedures that need to be carried out and who should carry them out? | | | |
| Additional risk assessments that may be required and who is responsible for carrying them out? | | | |
| Information on how health needs may affect the use of the service – e.g. transport issues? | | | |
| Supply, use, storage and maintenance of equipment? | | | |
| Individual preferences for how a procedure will be carried out? | | | |
| Anticipated changes? Arrangements for reviewing the plan? | | | |
| Do staff know where the plan/s are kept and can it be accessed by staff who need to read it? | | | |
| Are there arrangements in place that mean that the child or young person has a single plan or the plan drawn up by larger services are shared with smaller services as well as families who employ support staff? | | | |
| Where services are working with groups of children or young people, are strategies in place for summoning assistance in the case of emergencies? | | | |

| Positive behaviour support plans | Yes | In part | To be developed |
|---|---|---|---|
| Have key people, including parents and the young person themselves, been given the opportunity to feed into the plan? | | | |
| Has a functional assessment of the child's behaviour been carried out? | | | |

| | Yes | In part | To be developed |
|---|---|---|---|
| Does the plan cover proactive as well as reactive strategies? | | | |
| Is there a review process in place to ensure any learning from use of the reactive plan is captured and used to amend the plan? | | | |
| Has the young person had the plan explained to them and been given the opportunity to agree to it? | | | |

| Risk assessments and risk management | Yes | In part | To be developed |
|---|---|---|---|
| Have staff received training on risk management? | | | |
| Is there clarity on who should conduct the risk assessments? | | | |
| Are the risk assessments specific to the child and specific to a procedure? | | | |
| Are the risk assessments child-centred, balancing rights with risks and safeguarding the dignity of the child or young person? | | | |
| Does risk management relating to moving and handling consider the use of equipment that is appropriate to the service and encourages as much independence as possible? | | | |
| Have families who are employing personal assistants and other support staff been given training and access to their child's risk assessments so that they can put in place the necessary risk assessments expected of employers? | | | |

| Training | Yes | In part | To be developed |
|---|---|---|---|
| Are there opportunities for parents and staff to undertake training on positive behaviour support together? | | | |

| | Yes | In part | To be developed |
|---|---|---|---|
| Are there opportunities for staff to undertake awareness raising training around why challenging behaviour occurs and the key principles of behaviour management? | | | |
| Have all staff who may be required to use restrictive physical interventions been trained by an accredited training organisation experienced on training on children and young people's issues? | | | |
| Where children rely on augmentative communication systems have staff been trained in that system? | | | |
| Moving and handling – is there clarity about who to contact when specific training for an individual child or young person is required? | | | |
| Is the training carried out by a trainer who is accredited and competent to work with the child or young person? (Training should preferably be provided by a professional who knows the child) | | | |
| Have staff been given written instructions for carrying out moving and handling tasks? | | | |
| Where equipment is used, have staff been trained to use that equipment? | | | |
| Intimate care – have staff been trained to carry out intimate care tasks? | | | |
| Have staff had safeguarding training that enables them to understand why children with behaviour that challenges may be more vulnerable to abuse? | | | |

| Written information | Yes | In part | To be developed |
|---|---|---|---|
| Does the service hold written information about the child or young person that is accessible to the staff working with that child – disability, likes and dislikes, method of communication, emergency contacts etc? | | | |

| | Yes | In part | To be developed |
|---|---|---|---|
| Where medication is given, either orally or via an enteral feeding tube, have dosages been verified by a doctor? | | n/a | n/a |
| Is there a process for responding to changes of dosages at short notice? | | | |

| Written records | Yes | In part | To be developed |
|---|---|---|---|
| Does the service record the administration of medication and the carrying out of clinical procedures? | | | |
| Where the child or young person takes a number of different medicines, has consideration been given to using a single record – agreed by all agencies and the family? | | | |
| Does the service have a protocol on recording and reporting errors in the administration of medication and other procedures? | | | |
| Does the service record the specific training received by support staff? | | | |
| Is the amount of paperwork completed by staff in proportion to the size of the service received? | | | |

| Review and monitoring | Yes | In part | To be developed |
|---|---|---|---|
| Are the clinical procedures, moving and handling and intimate care reviewed at each annual review? | | | |
| Are the plans updated as part of the annual review? | | | |
| Are the training needs of staff regularly reviewed and updated? | | | |

# Acknowledgements

The Council for Disabled Children would like to thank the individuals and services listed below for sharing their examples of good practice, policy documents and forms and giving permission for them to be published in *Dignity and Inclusion: Making it work for children with behaviour that challenges.* These examples are provided to stimulate ideas and should assist services when writing policies and drawing up forms. We would recommend that local professionals, practitioners and families should be consulted and that all policies and forms should be appropriate to local circumstances and the nature and size of the service.

Abbey Court School, Medway

Barnardo's Brighton and Hove Link Plus Service

Barnardo's Cygnet Service

Barnardo's Hamara Project

Barnardo's Ravensdale Project

Barnardo's Sunrise Project

Brighton and Hove City Council Children's Services

Steve Broach, Luke Clements and Janet Read for the extract from Disabled Children: A legal handbook

Carers Trust

The Challenging Behaviour Foundation

The Children's Sleep Charity

Coventry City Council, Children's Disability Team

London Borough of Enfield's Joint Service for Disabled Children

Gloucestershire County Council, Family Link Service

Halton Positive Behaviour Support Service, Halton Borough Council and St Helen's and Halton Clinical Commissioning Groups

KIDS

National Autistic Society

Nottingham Children's Hospital

The Hub, Stopsley High School, Luton

Salford Safeguarding Children Board

Sussex Community NHS Trust

Torfield School, East Sussex

TreeHouse School, Ambitious About Autism, London

White Lodge Centre, Surrey

The Council for Disabled Children would also like to thank the individuals and organisations that gave so willingly of the time and expertise to be on the reference group for this publication:

- Joy Beaney, Torfield Inclusion Support Service and Torfield School
- Kay Al-Ghani, Torfield School
- Viv Cooper, Challenging Behaviour Foundation
- Beverley Dawkins, Mencap
- Karen Deacon, Young Epilepsy
- Gemma Honeyman, Challenging Behaviour Foundation
- Phil Howell, BILD
- Sharon Paley, BILD
- Antony Julyan, Triangle
- Susan Kelly, Short Breaks Network
- Ruth Watson, Barnardo's Hamara Project
- Kate Williams, Ambitious About Autism

And finally, thanks go to the expert readers who gave their comments on the volume during drafting:

Penny Barratt, The Bridge School, London

Mary Busk, Expert Parent

Louise Denne, Ambitious About Autism

Katy Lee, TreeHouse School, Ambitious About Autism

Wendy Lee, The Communications Trust

Pamela Shaw, Council for Disabled Children

Zara Todd, Council for Disabled Children

Ian Townsend, Advisory Teacher for Physical Impairment, Medway

Philippa Stobbs, Council for Disabled Children

Anna Gardiner, Council for Disabled Children